Darkes

and Television Industry Every Actor Should Know:

A Film Director and Actor Reveals Secrets for Your Acting, Auditions, Movie Roles and Self-Promotion

(plus How to Make Your Video for YouTube.com and Webisodes)

2nd Edition

Tom Marcoux

Feature Film Producer, Director, Actor and Screenwriter

Book #3 in the nine volume series
Darkest Secrets by Tom Marcoux

A QuickBreakthrough Publishing Edition

ISBN: 0615809340

ISBN-13: 978-0615809342

QuickBreakthrough Publishing is an imprint of Tom Marcoux Media, LLC. More copies are available from the publisher, Tom Marcoux Media, LLC. Please call (415) 572-6609 or write TomSuperCoach@gmail.com

or visit www.TomSuperCoach.com

or Tom's blog: www.BeHeardandBeTrusted.com

This book was developed and written with care. Names and details were modified to respect privacy.

Other Books by Tom Marcoux:

- Darkest Secrets of Charisma
- Darkest Secrets of Film Directing
- Darkest Secrets of Making a Pitch to the Film and Television Industry
- Darkest Secrets of Persuasion and Seduction Masters
- Darkest Secrets of Business Communication: Using Your Personal Brand
- Darkest Secrets of Small Business Marketing
- Darkest Secrets of Spiritual Seduction Masters
- Darkest Secrets of Negotiation Masters

Praise for *Darkest Secrets ... Every Actor Should Know:*

"The career strategies in this book can help new actors take hold of their own careers instead of waiting for the phone to ring."
– Danek S. Kaus, screenwriter and author of *Swords of the Dead*

"Are you wondering how to get work as an Actor? This book gives you the toolkit from acting skills to self promotion! Avoid small mistakes that cost you and can prevent you from getting a role you know you are right for. It even teaches you how to produce a video for YouTube or webisodes. As an actress, I really value this information. " – Carole Wilkinson

"When casting, film director Tom Marcoux's acting and improvisation skills shine as he works with actors."
– Daniel Buhlman, film director and actor

"Tom treats cast and crew with great respect. He listens to ideas. His support helped me express the truth in my scenes."
– David MacDowell Blue, actor, screenwriter and author of *The Annotated Carmilla*

Praise for Tom Marcoux's Other Work

"In *Darkest Secrets of Persuasion and Seduction Masters,* learn useful countermeasures to protect you from being darkly manipulated."
– David Barron, co-author, *Power Persuasion*

"In *Be Heard and Be Trusted,* Tom's advice on how to remain true to yourself and establish authentic rapport with clients is both insightful and reality based. He [shows how] to establish oneself as a credible expert."
-Arthur P. Ciaramicoli, Ed.D., Ph.D., author *The Curse of the Capable,* and *The Power of Empathy*

"*Nothing Can Stop You This Year* is a treasure trove of tips, tools, and terrific ideas—practical, reassuring, and energizing! Tom provides wonderful resources for achieving your goals." – Elayne Savage, Ph.D., author of *Don't Take It Personally! The Art of Dealing with Rejection*

Visit Tom's blog: www.BeHeardandBeTrusted.com

CONTENTS

DEDICATION AND ACKNOWLEDGEMENTS

This book is dedicated to the terrific book and film consultant, and author Johanna E. Mac Leod. It is also dedicated to the other team members. Thanks to David MacDowell Blue, Danek S. Kaus and Joan Harrison for editing. Thanks to my father, Al Marcoux, for his concern and efforts for me. Thanks to my mother, Sumiyo Marcoux, a kind, generous soul. Thanks to Daniel Buhlman for the cover photography and rendering this book's front cover. Thank you Johanna E. Mac Leod for rendering this book's back cover. Thank you to casting director Randi Acton for her insightful comments in the enclosed interview. Thank you to Higher Power. Thanks to our readers, audiences, clients, my graduate/college students and my team members of Tom Marcoux Media, LLC.

BOOK I: DARKEST SECRETS OF THE FILM AND TELEVISION INDUSTRY EVERY ACTOR SHOULD KNOW (AND YOUR COUNTERMEASURES) —CHAPTER 1

What do you really hope for with your acting career? Perhaps you want to feel the thrill of acting on the set of major feature films or in top productions on Broadway. Or you want to make top money appearing in television shows. Maybe you simply enjoy the adventure of expressing emotion as a variety of characters. Perhaps you continue to feel the hunger to perform since you were a teen.

Imagine that you could learn the real pitfalls and effective countermeasures to the tough parts of an acting career. Those answers wait within the pages of this book.

This book reveals *21 Darkest Secrets of the Film and Television Industry Every Actor Should Know*. More than that, it provides you with countermeasures so you'll do the right things to protect your career and leap forward to make your dreams come true. The section Book II provides a guide for producing and directing your own video for YouTube.com and webisodes. Producing your own short video helps you get essential demonstration footage (that helps one gain acting roles). Book III provides 25 secrets to self-promotion.

How did I come to write this book? As an actor and director of feature films and other work I have been on both sides of the audition table. So I'll pull back the curtain and reveal what directors are thinking during your audition. One of the feature films I directed (and had a lead role in) went to the Cannes Film market and gained international distribution. I've acted in feature films, commercials and more (projects headlined by Chris O'Donnell, Ricardo Montalban, and others). And I've taught workshops on acting and self-promotion.

Some of my former college students posted messages at Facebook about how tough it was to endure the film and television industry. Some of them were even quitting. I wanted to help. You see, I currently teach public speaking and science fiction cinema/literature to graduate students and college students. So I did not have the chance to teach those former college students the material contained in this book.

And now I am here, as your coach, to help you strengthen yourself and to help you overcome pitfalls of an acting career so you keep pursuing your dreams.

Let's begin with the next chapter.

DARKEST SECRET #1: FILM AND TV PEOPLE HAVE LONG MEMORIES AND THEY GET EVEN

After I ran some auditions, I went to my receptionist and asked about how a particular actor "Samuel" treated her and other actors. She gave me the news about Samuel's crass behavior and how he belittled everyone in the waiting room. I added that to my other observations and necessarily crossed Samuel off the list.

When you come across as friendly and professional, you get more offers and opportunities to audition. But a number of actors walk around moody. One of my filmmaking colleagues, a producer, said, "We want professionals; we don't want babies."

Throughout this book, I'll reveal subtle mistakes actors can make, seemingly innocent actions that create manifestly wrong impressions. A director told a friend of mine about how an actor who had the role at the end of his audition—until he asked to drink from one of the casting directors' water bottles.

For more insight, here is an excerpt from an interview

with Casting Director Randi Acton.

Near the end of the interview, Randi reveals how some casting directors appear to "get even." In this interview, Randi speaks about parents and child actors. However, there is much that any actor can gain from the straight forward advice Randi gives.

Tom: What are ideal qualifications for parents of child actors?

Randi: Parents [and all actors] need to be cooperative. Just pleasant to work with. The entertainment business is extremely stressful and very long hours. Everybody on a production is tired. So when you come on the set you want to be [pleasant] . . .

Tom: If there's only one thing you can tell a child actor that will help her get the part, what is it?

Randi: Just be yourself. I tell kids that there are apples and oranges. And a director, in his head, is looking for an apple. You come in, and you're the most talented, gorgeous, most adorable, charismatic orange. He adores you, but you're not an apple. So, it's not personal. Kids really have to know that if you don't get cast, it doesn't mean you're not talented. It just means you're an orange instead of an apple. It's as simple as that. Sometimes, he's looking for an apple, and you really are an incredible orange, and all of a sudden, he switches in his mind: "I don't want an apple. I changed my mind. I want an orange." And you get the part.

Tom: That's what happened to me. In two feature films I have directed, the part was written as a boy. And a girl came in – and the role changed to a girl. Both times!

Randi: I remember! Because what you saw ended up being what you needed. But you didn't know it until you saw it.

Tom: Tell me about how parents help or hinder their children.

Randi: On one film project, we ended up with a [name actor's son]. It didn't matter that he was the well-known actor's son. "Joey" [not his real name] was just brilliant. So he got the part. . . [Then,] we get this girl that's just incredible. And even Joey said, "That's who I want." They had a relationship because they did callbacks together. Their chemistry together was incredible. So everything is perfect. Everything is great. They come to the set, and the girl turns into a complete nightmare. Her acting was brilliant. Her look was great. She became this overnight, stuck-up, little star at a young age. It was a major nightmare. The girl was difficult. Someone went up to her and asked, "What part are you playing?" She replied, "I'm the star!" It got to where we were sick to our stomachs. And her mother didn't handle that at all. Her mother was just as bad. There was a big fight between the mothers. . . I will never cast her again [as a child]. And I'm sure that the parents have no idea . . . . If the parents are difficult, I will not cast the kid again. We have enough headaches and enough emergency things to deal with. We want to work with actors that are easy to work with. I'd take an actor that is easy to work with even over a talented actor that's a snob. On another film, an adult was complaining about the size of her trailer. She made it a big problem. She was calling her manager . . . She is famous, but I won't cast her again. I won't put up with that. There are too many nice people in the world, who are also talented and not stuck up. I've talked with other casting directors, and most of us don't put up with that."

[The rest of the interview with Casting Director Randi Acton is in Book IV of this book.]

* * *

At Hollywood gatherings, I have repeatedly heard a number of people saying: "I won't put up with that." Casting directors say, "I won't work with that actor again. I won't put up with that." And I hear actors say, "I finally fired my agent." Film industry people, under so much pressure, seek to relieve it by avoiding people who rub them the wrong way.

For example, Ed Harris, while acting in James Cameron's *The Abyss* nicknamed the film "The Abuse." Ed said that he felt traumatized from the filmmaking and found himself crying in the car on his way back to the hotel. Ed also said that he would never again work with James Cameron.

Earlier I spoke of film and television people having long memories. In 1999, George Clooney had an argument with director David O. Russell on the set of *Three Kings*. The words led to punches. To this day, George Clooney maintains that he will never work with Russell again.

As I discuss the Darkest Secrets in this book, every section will include countermeasures so that you do the right things for your own career. For example, one countermeasure for this section is: avoid causing directors, producers and casting people problems. Make sure to have some positive interactions.

Directors, producers and casting people only like to hire people who make their lives easier.

For example, Steven Spielberg made the following movies with Michael Kahn as his editor: *Lincoln, The Adventures of Tintin, Indiana Jones and the Kingdom of the Crystal Skull, Munich, War of the Worlds, The Terminal, Catch Me if You Can, Minority Report, A.I, Artificial Intelligence, Saving Private Ryan,*

Amistad, The Lost World: Jurassic Park, Schindler's List, Jurassic Park, Hook, Always, Indiana Jones and the Last Crusade, Empire of the Sun, The Color Purple, Indiana Jones and the Temple of Doom, Raiders of the Lost Ark, 1941, and *Close Encounters of the Third Kind.*

Steven Spielberg enlisted John Williams as the composer of the music soundtracks for all of the above films except *The Color Purple.*

Points to Remember:

- **Darkest Secret #1: Film and TV people have long memories and they get even.**

- **Your Countermeasure:**

Avoid causing directors, producers and casting people problems. Make some friends or at least have some positive interactions. Remember, film and television people are extremely busy, stressed out and tired people. They label co-workers quickly. They only like to hire people who make their lives easier.

CHAPTER 2
DARKEST SECRET #2: YOU CAN'T "GET IN" THE INDUSTRY UNTIL YOU PROVE YOURSELF (BUT YOU CAN TAKE MATTERS INTO YOUR OWN HANDS)

Industry people talk about how, in many cases, you can't get significant roles in film and television unless you're a SAG actor (Screen Actors Guild) or have an agent. However, many agents don't look at actors who are not with SAG. This is an apparent Catch-22.

There is a solution to the above conundrum. Do something, in a small way, that demonstrates your skill (which can lead to roles in independent films and more). Numerous people are using the Internet, and YouTube.com in particular, to gain attention and jump start their careers. For example, singer/songwriter Dave Carroll felt both injury and insult when United Airlines baggage handlers broke his guitar. United Airlines personnel said that the company would not make restitution. Dave replied that if they did not fix his guitar, he would make and post three music videos on YouTube. The videos would expose the problems of the broken guitar and his disappointment about United's refusal to fix the guitar. As of this writing, the music video and song "United Breaks Guitars" has had 13,006,164 views on YouTube.com. It is likely that Dave Carroll has gotten a lot of gigs due to the video. He even authored a book titled *United Breaks Guitars: The Power of One Voice in the Age of Social Media.*

Actress Felicia Day took action and created a webisodes series entitled *The Guild.* And this action led to her starring in at least 13 episodes of the TV Series *Eureka.* Here's how she describes the process (at her website):

"There are a few times in life when you REALLY get rewarded for working hard. That is the story of why I am playing 'Dr. Holly Martin' on *Eureka* [TV series]. The exec producer Amy Berg and showrunner Jamie Paglia were aware of my work on the web (because they are awesome, true geeks themselves) and they actually CREATED this role for me. Yep, no Hollywood agents, no horrific auditions where I cry in the car afterwards, they simply called me in for a meeting and basically created the funnest character I've ever played. And KEPT writing her in! The great thing about Eureka is that it's a wonderful balance of quirky comedy and drama, the exact tone and sensibility I love to play. And the crew is truly wonderful. So seriously, it couldn't be a bigger dream come true to be flying back and forth to Vancouver and playing around with what I like to call my Canadian family now. As of this writing, I've done 13 episodes over seasons 4 and 5."

Regarding Felicia Day's web series *The Guild:*
"*The Guild* [now in its fifth season] is a independent

sitcom web series about a group of online gamers. The show started in the late summer of 2007, and for the first season was financed solely by PayPal donations from LOYAL FANS. Since season 2, The Guild has been distributed by Xbox Live and Microsoft and sponsored by Sprint. Episodes vary from 3-8 minutes in length, and follow the Guild members' lives online and offline. "The Guild" has won numerous awards, including the SXSW, YouTube and Yahoo Web Series Awards in 2008, and 3 Streamy Awards in 2009: Best Comedy Web Series, Best Ensemble, and Best Actress for Felicia Day." [from watchtheguild.com]

Years ago, Billy Bob Thornton proved to the film industry that he could act when he wrote, directed and starred in the feature film *Sling Blade.* Similarly, Bruce Campbell produced and starred in the first low budget feature film *The Evil Dead,* which was directed by his friend Sam Raimi. Bruce's career took off after that first feature film led to two sequels, television show guest appearances, playing the lead in the TV series *The Adventures of Brisco County, Jr.,* and leading roles in other feature films. Currently, Bruce co-stars on the hit TV series *Burn Notice.*

The above four examples reveal that you can do something to forward your career. You can cast yourself. Produce your own short film first. And consider producing your own web series or feature film.

To demonstrate your acting skills (and simultaneously improve them), you could produce short films and place them on YouTube.com and you can embed the films on a page at your own actor website. In a later section of this book entitled *BOOK II: Taking Control of Your Career: Producing Your Own Short Film, Feature Film or Web Series,* I will share numerous strategies that my colleagues and I have developed through hard-won experience.

Points to Remember:

- **Darkest Secret #2: You can't "get in" the industry until you prove yourself (but you can take matters into your own hands).**

- **Your Countermeasure:**

Take your career into your own hands. Cast yourself and produce a short film for YouTube.com and your demo reel. You could do a 30 second commercial for a film that features you in a role that you feel is a perfect match for you. Consider producing a low-budget feature film (or webisodes series) and cast yourself.

CHAPTER 3
DARKEST SECRET #3: FILM AND TV PEOPLE MAKE THINGS "COMPLICATED," BUT SIMPLICITY CAN POWER UP YOUR CAREER

Actors and directors may take up a lot of time talking about motivation, objective, the Method and more. That's not necessarily bad.

But for you to be an effective and working actor, cut to the chase. Find the essence of the character. Find the simple key to your character.

Christopher Reeve (who portrayed Superman in the feature film and subsequently earned a star on the Hollywood Walk of Fame) said, "When Lois Lane asks, 'Who are you?' Superman simply responds, 'A friend.' I felt that was the key to the part: I tried to downplay being a hero and emphasized being a friend."

Often, top actors mention that they boil down the character to one simple sentence. Dustin Hoffman worked (and pushed) director Sydney Pollack as he struggled to improve the screenplay of *Tootsie* with a series of writers. Finally, they were able to get to the simple truth of the screenplay: "A man becomes a better man by portraying a woman."

Since I mentioned Christopher Reeve, let's also learn some life lessons that he shared:

"I think a hero is an ordinary individual who finds the strength to persevere and endure in spite of overwhelming obstacles." Certainly, being a working actor involves the tough obstacles of rejection, disappointment, and trying to keep food on the table.

Christopher Reeve talked about being a hero from his wheelchair, from where he had transformed his personal paralysis into his quest to increase funding toward curing spinal cord injuries. About the fall off a horse he suffered, Chris said, "If I made a mistake, I've got to forgive myself for being human."

From Chris, we also learn to forgive ourselves for being human. Every actor, including me, comes out of auditions thinking, "Oh, what a mistake! I shouldn't have done that!" I advise actors to write down in their diary: 1) items I did well and 2) areas to improve. In essence, you praise yourself with the "I did well" section and you make observations (like your own coach) with "areas to improve" section. Then you close your diary and feel free to go on with your day. You have done your job.

Let's discuss using simplicity to help your acting performance.

Your Countermeasure:

Use the simplicity of 'Stanislavski's Physical Actions.'

Konstantin S. Stanislavski developed a system for the professional training of an actor. For years, Stanislavski's method was referred to when someone said, "he's a method actor." Sonia Moore, the author of *The Stanislavski System:*

The Professional Training of an Actor summarizes how physical actions are important to great acting:

"...a truthfully executed simple physical action justified by the given moment and connected with the needed emotion will involve [the actor's] psychophysical apparatus and make his faculties function: his truthful emotions in the given circumstances will appear, and he will be introduced naturally into the inner experiences of the character he portrays."

Here's an example. In one feature film, I portrayed a character "David." In one scene, his ex-wife confronts David and vividly reminds him of something for which he feels deeply ashamed. As an actor, I pulled an emotional memory. I remembered the pain and emptiness I felt in my chest upon the ending of a two-and-a-half year romantic relationship. Back then, in real life, my right hand went to my chest. And while acting in the scene, I used that simple physical action. In preparing for auditions, develop your own tool kit of emotional memories and "simple physical actions."

Below we'll use a *Get the Part Tool Kit for Auditions* worksheet. Before you attend an audition, review your completed worksheet. In the worksheet, I will present you with an improvisation situation. Then I will provide you with an objective. I'll ask you to uncover your appropriate emotional memory. Finally, I will invite you to discover a physical action.

Here is an example:

Emotion: Desperation and loneliness

Improvisation: In the (empty) chair is your (the character's) father.

Your objective: "I want to AWAKEN my father's love for me."

Your emotional memory: "A time when a sweetheart was

angry and shut me out."

Your simple physical action: Your left hand is trying to reach out and touch her shoulder—but feeling an emptiness and closing in pain.

I am designing these improvisations for you to act toward an empty chair. The reason is that often you are auditioning with a reader who is giving you nothing. You need to use your own imagination to create the truth of the scene.

Worksheet for Developing Physical Action—
Your Get-the-Part Tool Kit for Auditions

1. Emotion: Desperation and loneliness

Improvisation: In the (empty) chair is your (the character's) father.

Your objective: I want to AWAKEN my father's love for me.

Your emotional memory:

Your simple physical action:

2. Emotion: Excitement

Improvisation: In the (empty) chair is your lover.

Your objective: I want to PERSUADE my lover to say yes to my favorite vacation spot.

Your emotional memory:

Your simple physical action:

3. Emotion: Sadness

Improvisation: In the (empty) chair is your dearest friend who is dying.

Your objective: I want to CONVINCE her of my pain so that she won't leave and die.

Your emotional memory:
Your simple physical action:

4. Emotion: Anger

Improvisation: In the (empty) chair is your co-worker who lied and got you fired.

Your objective: I want to OVERWHELM my co-worker into feeling horrible and telling the truth to my boss.

Your emotional memory:
Your simple physical action:

5. Emotion: Love

Improvisation: In the (empty) chair is your lover.

Your objective: I want to TAKE CARE of my lover and have her FEEL my love.

Your emotional memory:
Your simple physical action:

6. Emotion: Courage

Improvisation: The chair represents a huge bear. You have only a small homemade spear.

Your objective: I want to KILL this bear and protect my small daughter.

Your emotional memory:
Your simple physical action:

* * *

We have discussed two ways to use simplicity to improve your acting performance: a) use a key line of dialogue and b) use a simple physical action. Simplicity can be a springboard for you to get to the essence of your character.

Points to Remember:

- **Darkest Secret #3: Film and TV people make things "complicated," but simplicity can power up your career.**

- **Your Countermeasure:**

Look for the simple key to your character. Also consider using Stanislavski's simple physical action method to enhance your acting.

CHAPTER 4
DARKEST SECRET #4: PEOPLE SAY THEY HATE BAD ACTING/OVERACTING BUT THEY HATE "BLAND" ACTING EVEN MORE

I learned this one the hard way as an actor during an audition. The feature film director called for a Southern accent. I'm Asian American and I was afraid of overacting so I did a light accent. Only days afterward, did I realize that I would have been better off doing a "big accent" and then backing off by saying something like: "I have a lot of range [said with a big accent] and maybe you'd like me to back off the accent [delivered with a diminishing accent]."

I did not get the role.

As a director, I like actors who offer a lot of choices and demonstrate that they're flexible.

You need to show definite changes in your performance—that's how a director knows that that you take direction well. Some directors say something like: "I can rein an actor in, but I can't do anything if there's nothing there."

I discussed "bland acting" with a number of friends who are actors. One said, "You're touching on a basic conundrum of acting. The essence of good acting is truth, honesty, often simplicity—but at the same time actors need to be interesting. I once saw a major production on Broadway, by a Pulitzer Prize-winning playwright. The lead was a genuinely major star of stage and screen, deservedly so, a renowned actor. Yet the actor opposite him was so ordinary, so low energy, she basically sucked the energy out of his performance. In trying to react with her, his own acting suffered. She was naturalistic, but she wasn't also larger-than-life. I had an acting teacher who said that to become an actor means you sign a pact . . . that says you cannot be ordinary at all. Everything you do must be fascinating. And yet, totally grounded. Threading that needle is the great trick of acting. Too many cannot manage it. What they end up being is cutesy or bombastic or just fast and loud."

I'll add that it may take a few years to find your stride. Some actors find their stride by being unusual. Think of William Shatner or Samuel Jackson (who always has an "angry scene"). These two actors have found their personal niche that works for them so well that their careers span decades.

Most working actors are not leading men and women. See almost any major film or most television shows that last for any length of time and you see faces you recognize. What are their names? You probably don't know. But the casting director knows their names. And the accountant who cuts the checks!

Those roles can also lead to places. Jennifer Anniston was on six or seven different TV shows (some of them quite good) that crashed and burned. She simply assumed that Friends would be the next on the list. Instead she ended up a star and a millionaire.

My point is that you need to stay in the game. Noriyuki "Pat" Morita went from a tiny part in a feature film Thoroughly Modern Millie to, 17 years later, the role of Mr. Miyagi in *The Karate Kid* movie series, for which he was nominated for the Academy Award for Best Supporting Actor in 1984. Pat Morita was 52 years old when the big success of the Mr. Miyagi role arrived. He portrayed the character in four films, which culminated in *The Next Karate Kid*, which provided Hilary Swank's first major role. Hilary Swank went on to win the Academy Award for Best Actress twice, as Brandon Teena in *Boys Don't Cry* (1999) and as a struggling waitress-turned-boxer Maggie Fitzgerald in *Million Dollar Baby* (2004).

Points to Remember:

- **Darkest Secret #4: People say they hate bad acting/overacting but they hate "bland" acting even more.**

- **Your Countermeasure:**

Offer the director a number of choices. And demonstrate your range. You can do it by talking about what you're doing. You can say, "I'll start with a heavy accent, and now I'll lighten the accent [for example]." Make sure that the director sees that her direction has significantly changed your performance.

CHAPTER 5

DARKEST SECRET #5: FILM AND TV PEOPLE EXPECT YOU TO TREAT THEM LIKE THEY'RE SPECIAL, AND TO GET BACK TO THEM FAST (BUT THEY WON'T DO THE SAME FOR YOU)

Make sure you check your email for messages often. The same with your LinkedIn account and Facebook account. Film industry people expect you to be quick with responses.

It may take months or years to get a film funded or set up at a studio, but then it's rush-rush-rush. Why? People want to get everything in place because they fear that somehow a studio executive may pull the plug on the project. So casting may come together quickly and at the last minute. For example, for the film *Aliens*, actor Michael Biehn got a phone call on a Friday night requesting he take over the role of Hicks, and he was in London to start filming on the following Monday.

Michael Biehn got a phone call, but now you could get a summons to audition through email or text message or via a message at Facebook or Linkedin.com [or some other social media service you use]. You must be responsive because you may get a role when some other actor does not work for the production.

Eric Stolz was not working as director Robert Zemeckis had intended for his film *Back to the Future.* He told Steven Spielberg about his concerns. Later, Spielberg said, "Bob showed me the first five weeks of shooting that he had put together. And [Bob] said, 'I just don't think we're getting the laughs I was hoping we would get.'"

They made the decision to replace Eric with Michael J. Fox to the loss of $4 million required for all the reshoots. $4 million in 1980's dollars was a lot of money.

Film directors and producers expect to be treated like they're special. How do you do that? First, you make sure that you are accessible and that you check your voicemail, email, LinkedIn account, and Facebook a lot. It is unlikely that you'll get a formal summons to an audition through LinkedIn or Facebook, but people expect to get timely replies to messages left with either service.

Second, you anticipate their needs and show how you, as an excellent professional, will be an asset to the production.

Your Countermeasure: Think ahead and make life easy for the other person.

For example, it would do you a lot of good to think about what a film director really needs.

Target the Director's Six Top Requirements

What is the director really looking for? In his book *The Director's Journey: The Creative Collaboration between Directors, Writers & Actors,* film director Mark W. Travis emphasizes that the director needs to watch for the actor's...

"1. Script comprehension
2. Courage
3. Originality
4. Clarity of objectives, character arc
5. Selflessness
6. Honesty"

Let's look at this process from the actor's perspective. That is, here are the categories and questions you can ask yourself:

1. Script comprehension

Are you showing that you understand the script? And that you have a good storytelling sense?

2. Courage

Do you show that you're making bold choices with how you're portraying the character? Director Francis Ford Coppola spoke of how Marlon Brando made choices to transform himself from an actor in his 40's to the character Don Corleone (in his 60's) in *The Godfather*. Brando said that he saw the character as having the face of a bull dog and he stuck tissues in his mouth to fill out his cheeks, during a first screen test. When you make bold choices you can often bring unpredictability and freshness to the material.

3. Originality

Are you showing unique choices instead of playing it safe?

4. Clarity of objectives, character arc

Do you help the audience feel that your choices are clear and that your choices are the only logical choices?

5. Selflessness

Do you show that you're "giving"? Mark Travis warns directors to beware of "actors who require high maintenance [because they] can literally suck the energy out of everyone."

6. Honesty

No matter what the material, do you generate a sense of truth and a feeling of reality?

Now, I'll share examples from auditions I have run for my motion pictures:

1. Script comprehension

For one of my feature films, the scene had "David" explaining the presence of a drunk man sleeping on their living room floor. The character "David" implores his girlfriend to be understanding as he says, "Come on, Laura, he needs help." One auditioning actress said the next line "He's not the only one" with just the right tone. In fact, it made the others in the room laugh. She demonstrated that she understood the line. She got the part!

2. Courage

When I ran the audition for my upcoming science fiction feature film *TimePulse*, one actress made a bold choice. The scene called for her character to have an injury to some 'tentacles' coming from her wrist (It is science fiction…). She yelled as if her arm was broken. That was a bold choice, and it startled her scene partner. I paid extra attention because I didn't know what she was going to do next. This was the same kind of wonderful, unpredictable energy that James Dean and Marlon Brando expressed years ago.

3. Originality

During a *TimePulse* audition, one female actor ad-libbed some unusual lines after I invited her to chastise her scene partner. She ad-libbed: "Is that it?! You stare at my bum (a British expression for buttocks), but when I really need you, you don't…." She captured our attention.

4. Clarity of objectives, character arc

During an audition for one of my films, one actor showed a mastery of beat changes. He began the speech with quiet intensity and worked up to anguish. You could tell that the character was coming to a personal catharsis of releasing inner demons. You could see the character arc coming to fruition.

5. Selflessness

During a *TimePulse* audition, one actor demonstrated the opposite of selflessness. She keep kicking and approaching her scene partner – attempting to show off her prowess. She put her partner in jeopardy. And we put her headshot in the "not suitable pile."

6. Honesty

During a *TimePulse* audition, one female actor put so much heart and intensity into her monologue. She used lines from some fantasy film: "You killed my family and burned our village. I have come for you…" The lines may have had clichés, but her eyes were on fire. She believed in what she was saying–and the casting team did, too!

To "treat a director as special," you need to prepare for the audition and think through what she needs before you get there. Remember the director's six top requirements and preplan how you will show that you meet them.

Points to Remember:

• **Darkest Secret #5: Film and TV people expect you to treat them like they're special, and to get back to them fast. (But they won't do the same for you.)**

• **Your Countermeasure:**

Be sure to monitor your voicemail, email and social media accounts at Facebook and Linkedin.com. Respond quickly. In business, the first responder often gets the job.

During an audition also make sure to demonstrate how you fulfill the Director's Six Requirements:

1. Script comprehension
2. Courage
3. Originality
4. Clarity of objectives, character arc
5. Selflessness
6. Honesty

CHAPTER 6
DARKEST SECRET #6: NO MATTER WHAT YOU HAVE DONE FOR THEM, A FILM OR TV PERSON WILL QUICKLY WRITE YOU OFF AS "DIFFICULT," UNTRUSTWORTHY OR "UNPROFESSIONAL"—IF SOMETHING RUBS THEM THE WRONG WAY.

A reputation may take years to make and be destroyed in five minutes. The well-regarded actor comes into an audition prepared and comfortable.

Your Countermeasure:
Increase Your Comfort and Work with Beat Changes and Your Objective

A successful actor increases her comfort by preparing herself for acting situations. For example, Paul Newman had in his contract a necessary two weeks rehearsal period before production of any feature film he agreed to star in. Paul said,

"The studio likes this because I give my time for free [during those two weeks]." How does the successful actor rehearse for auditions? She uses each audition as a rehearsal for the next audition. She also rehearses and prepares for the audition requirements. In an audition you are usually asked to do the following audition activities:

1) Cold read (you've never seen the script, and you're expected to give some form of a good performance as you read it)
2) Improvise
3) Quickly find the beats (changes in tempo, tone, and emotion)
4) Give "more"
5) Give "less"

The successful actor practices all five actions.

What the Film Director is Thinking (about the Actor's Comfort During an Audition)

The director is looking for a professional actor. The director has thoughts like: "I realize that an audition is stressful. But acting on the set is stressful, too. Does this actor have the concentration skills? Can she make herself comfortable? Especially when I need to be elsewhere, focusing on a technical problem?"

Here are two ways you can increase your comfort during the audition by finding the beats and the objective of the character.

Method #1: Find the beats in the script quickly
(Do a better cold reading).
Increase your comfort in doing cold readings by learning

the process of identifying and expressing beat changes (changes in tempo, tone and mood at a specific dramatic moment). The following speech is from a screenplay I wrote for a feature film I directed:

JOHN

That year I spent in 'Nam. I met a girl.
She was so beautiful. I was eighteen years old.
and we were going to be married. But then Saigon
fell, and I lost her—and our baby. I finally found
them in a refugee camp. But Kim got sick.... And
Kim...died.
(begins crying)
...God...

You increase your comfort when you practice coming up with the beat changes. When you show smooth beat changes, you show that you're a good actor.

Now, let's break this speech down:

JOHN: "That year I spent in 'Nam."[probably mixed feelings. Some pain. Some horror. But this is the beginning of this section, so I'll give a 'hint' of it]

"I met a girl. She was so beautiful. I was eighteen years old, and we were going to be married." [These lines feel like happy memory time. I'll be in the moment, and feel the happy times.]

"But then Saigon fell, and I lost her – and our baby." [Here's a big transition. When I start happy, then I can come crashing down at this point.]

"I finally found them in a refugee camp." [Here's a moment of lightness – possible hope.]

"But Kim got sick.... And Kim...died. (begins crying)...God...."
[Here's the final plunge into heart-searing pain...]

So we've uncovered five strong beat changes. Are these the correct ones? When you're auditioning you don't know. It's also possible that the director doesn't know yet. It's most important that you make definite, strong choices. If the director wants to see you try something else, she'll tell you.

Increase your comfort by getting together with a friend who is an actor. Have her choose a script that you do not know. Give a 'cold reading' in front of her. This is how you rehearse for auditions. Now, have her do a "cold reading" for you. See how you both find beat changes.

Method #2: Identify the objective of your character quickly
(Do a better cold reading)

William Ball, founder of American Conservatory Theatre, emphasized the objective of the character. Here are three of his examples:

Verb - Receiver - Desired Response
I want... to WIN... Gloria's... admiration.
I want... to IGNITE... the crowd... to riot.
I want... to PERSUADE... Ann... to kiss me.

So let's now go back to John's speech from my screenplay.

JOHN

That year I spent in 'Nam. I met a girl.
She was so beautiful. I was eighteen years old.
and we were going to be married. But then Saigon
fell, and I lost her—and our baby. I finally found
them in a refugee camp. But Kim got sick.... And
Kim...died.
(begins crying)
...God...

What is John's objective? Good question. If pages are available, look backwards in the script.

Here's more pages of the screenplay:

SON (CONT'D)

...The mother couldn't live. We had to
help put her into the water. Baby cry. She
never see Momma again. I can't help them.
I can't help you.

JOHN

That year I spent in 'Nam. I met a girl.
She was so beautiful. I was eighteen years old.
and we were going to be married. But then Saigon
fell, and I lost her—and our baby. I finally found
them in a refugee camp. But Kim got sick.... And
Kim...died.
(begins crying)
...God...

So John's objective could be:

[remember the pattern: Verb - Receiver - Desired Response]

I want… to EXPRESS my story to Son….. to make him stop pushing me to talk.

(OR)

I want… to RELEASE my story to Son…. so I begin to heal.

Often, during auditions I run for my feature films, I ask the actor, "What is the action of this scene?" I'm really talking about objectives.

Again, this involves practice. Increase your comfort level by getting together with a friend who is an actor. Have her choose a script that you do not know. Give a cold reading in front of her. Now, she asks what is the objective of your character.

Practice responding. This is how you rehearse for auditions. Now, have her do a cold reading for you. See how you both find objectives for your characters.

Three Ways to Handle Butterflies in the Stomach

Many of us have felt that unsettled feeling in our stomachs known as butterflies.

A successful actor handles butterflies in the stomach by "falling back on the craft of acting." For example, director James Cameron found a director's dream in Kate Winslet during her audition for the part of Rose in *Titanic*. Later, James said, "From a performance standpoint, [Kate was] very, very flexible. She could take any idea and juggle it, integrate it, and something interesting would come of it. And we were having fun. It was exhausting, but it was fun." James Cameron ran a polished screen test for Titanic with Kate Winslet in full period wardrobe – and lighting by True Lies director of photography Russell Carpenter.

James Cameron said, "I was looking for a chemistry between the director and the actor. I wanted somebody [to play Rose] that could act as a conduit for our present-day emotions, who would be from that time and still be just like us. Rose [is an] Audrey Hepburn type: spunky, smart, and elegant."

Master actor Sir John Gielgud wrote, "Many lessons in the theater [are] to be learned: application, concentration, self-discipline, the use of the voice and body, imagination, observation, simplification, self-criticism....One's basic technical equipment should be perfected in order to enable one to relax, to simplify, to cut away dead wood."

So how do we do that? We get training, and we simply get out there and do it. Get in front of the camera as much as possible. Participate in many auditions. Do student films. Act in small independent films—even for a deferred salary (everyone is paid when the film sells). Independent films have significant visibility. In addition to print-on-demand video on Amazon.com, old standbys continue. Robert Redford's Sundance Film Festival and Sundance Cinemas (San Francisco, CA; Houston, TX; and Madison, WI) experience continued success. The Sundance Channel and the Independent Film Channel are still going strong.

What the Director is Thinking (about the Actor and butterflies in her stomach)

When a director sees an actor who is tense, she wonders, "Does this actor know muscle tension release methods? Will this actor be tense on my set? Can I count on this actor to perform consistently?" The best way to let go of the preoccupation of 'how am I doing' is to focus in the moment. Concentrate on listening. Henry Fonda (star of *On Golden Pond* with Katherine Hepburn and Jane Fonda) said, "Acting is reacting."

Concentrate on being in the moment and going with your instincts. Make definite choices.

Here are three methods for dealing with butterflies in the stomach.

1. Use the feeling as preparation energy.

Even seasoned and well-received actors often have butterflies in the stomach. What they do is use the feeling as preparation energy. They may rehearse their lines a bit more in their dressing rooms. They may use the feeling as a signal to do some deep breathing.

Having the butterflies fly in formation is to accept the feelings' presence and to use the energy. Speakers often note that the feelings of fear and excitement are similar. They often advise that you acknowledge your feeling, perhaps saying to yourself, "Okay, I hear you." Then, convert the fear to excitement by saying in your mind, "I am excited about the possibilities." When you're in the waiting room, go over your lines, then close your eyes.

Researchers have found that by closing your eyes you cut down 80% of the environment's impact on you. Close your eyes and concentrate. In your personal journal, note what you can tell yourself that will help you convert the fear into excitement.

2. Pre-plan your responses.

Here are audition scenarios and ways to respond effectively:

a. You meet someone in the waiting room:
Respond: "Hi, I'm ___ and you are....?"

b. The director says, "Tell me about yourself..."
Respond:

- Name two of your best credits…
- Name two interesting skills you have. Here are examples: "I'm a martial artist; I have military training; I was a police officer; I volunteer with children; 'I've learned…'"

Now, it's your turn. Pull out your personal journal and pre-plan how you would prefer to respond to audition scenarios.

3. Practice your responses.

Practice with a friend. If a friend is not handy, practice with an audio recorder. Using a audio recorder helps me get into the proper state of being—because when I turn on the audio recorder, I feel like I'm on stage. Using the audio recorder to ramp up my energy is in line with research in state dependent learning. If my adrenaline is flowing when I turn on the audio recorder, then I'll be ready when my adrenaline is flowing during a critical audition. In your personal journal, name two friends you can practice with and make a plan to use an audio recorder.

Use Six Methods to Avoid Audition Mistakes

Leonardo DiCaprio refused to do an audition (at first) for Director James Cameron for *Titanic*. Now, refusing to audition seems like a real mistake. And it could have destroyed his opportunity to play Jack Dawson in *Titanic*. But Leo was lucky. James Cameron said, "Leo read the scene once, and then he got up and started goofing around...but for one split second, a shaft of light came down from the heavens and lit up the forest."

I mention this example because even big mistakes can be overcome. DiCaprio also had other things going for him. For example, something happened when Cameron first met Leo at an informal meeting at his Lightstorm company offices. When Cameron arrived late, he discovered that almost every female Lightstorm team member was in the conference room with DiCaprio. Cameron said, "Leo must be used to this because he charmed everyone in the room."

One week later, right after auditioning with Leo, Kate Winslet ('Rose') pulled James Cameron aside and told him, "Even if you don't hire me, you have to hire [Leo]."

James Cameron found Leo "incredibly mercurial." Leo would run ten different emotions through a scene. When 20th Century Fox executives were not sold on Leo to star in Titanic (even though they were seeing dailies of Leo's film *Romeo+Juliet*), James Cameron said, "I always trust my first impression. It sounds corny, but that's what the audience does."

What the Director is Thinking (about Audition Mistakes)

A director wants someone who is flexible and adaptable. The director realizes that you don't have a full script in front of you. But she'll take tentativeness or hesitation on your part as being "green at acting." So it's best to make definite choices. The director will often say, "Give me more of ____" or "Give me less of _____." Then, make the change. But don't make it a subtle one, because the director is looking for the difference.

Also become known as a cooperative actor. For example, Sean Connery let go of many usual "star" accommodations for his feature film *Entrapment*, creating a $2 million savings. Entrapment was completed for $66 million. Sean said, "I think you should respect the parent company." Recently, Johnny Depp and director Gore Verbinski agreed to several changes so that the budget for *The Lone Ranger* was reduced from $250 million to $215 million. Some people may think that the change was not that much. But in a negotiation (even over a movie budget), the other side often just wants to see positive "movement."

To continue with the theme of "being flexible," make sure you prepare so you can adapt to things that happen in auditions. You'll want to avoid these Audition Mistakes:

1) Appearing negative
2) Appearing needy
3) Appearing arrogant
4) Appearing unsure—like you lack confidence and seem to have nothing to offer
5) appearing unresponsive

Your Countermeasures: Use the following six methods to avoid mistakes that sour your audition.

Method #1: Talk in positive ways

(avoid appearing negative).

Don't complain about traffic you endured on the way to the audition—or anything. If the director asks about another project you were in, only say positive things like: "I appreciated the opportunity to play that character. I learned some new things."

Method #2: Use Self-Care Methods

(avoid appearing "needy").

Don't complain about another actor or a previous director. If you feel depressed or angry about anything, find a safe place to vent. Perhaps vent with a counselor, trustworthy friend, or support group. Avoid venting in professional situations. Avoid getting the reputation as a "high maintenance" actor. Directors' lives are filled with problems, and they avoid "problem actors"' as much as possible. Director Martin Ritt of *Nuts* (starring Barbra Streisand and Richard Dreyfus) said that he would never work with Barbra Streisand again.

Method #3: Project Warm Confidence
(avoid appearing arrogant).

Smile. Avoid comments like: "Will we be going in order? I have another appointment" or "How long will this take?" The director feels that her film is the most important part of your day. So don't say anything that indicates that you feel otherwise.

Method #4: Move and Talk with Confidence
(avoid appearing unsure–like you have nothing to offer).

Smile. Confident people always offer their name first. You can say your name and then ask for the person's name in this manner: "Hello, I'm Sarah Avegard, and you are . . .?" Confident people walk with poise. Often, directors or other casting decision-makers will say, "So tell me about yourself." So it is important to write out your 25-second biography and memorize your lines. Here's an example of a 25-second biography:

"My journey to portraying strong female characters began when I was 9 years old and I punched Sam Stoden when he threatened my little brother. Since that time, I've studied karate, kung fu, and judo and I completed one year of the police academy when I got my first role in the feature film *One Rough Night . . .*"

Now, it's your turn. Take out a sheet of paper or your personal journal and list two of your best credits. List two things about yourself that make you interesting (examples: police officer; volunteer with children; volunteer with elderly people; other ideas).

Method #5: Make Definite Choices

(avoid appearing unresponsive).

Many actors are deathly afraid of overacting. However, if you're auditioning and the director says, "Show me more frustration," then do not hold back! She's looking for your ability to take direction. She's looking for a change. So show her a change! Many directors are trained to ask: 1) "What are you trying to GET him to do?" and 2) "What are you trying to MAKE him do?" Find definite choices that answer these questions.

Method #6: Stay in rapport by noticing how the person takes in information

A major audition mistake is to break rapport. It's easy to do because we have our own internal monologue going 24/7. There's an old story of how a Hollywood actress monopolized a conversation, turning it into a monologue about her. She then said, "Enough about me. So how did you like my latest movie?" This actress was not paying attention to her listener.

You can build rapport with a new person by noticing how she responds to you. Researchers point out that each person has a preferred input style. That is, some of us like to learn about new things primarily through visual, auditory, or kinesthetic (touch) modes. For example, if I get a phone call from a salesperson who wants me to consider a new product, I ask if there's website for me to view because my preferred input style is visual.

How to Notice a Person's Preferred Input Style

a) Does the person say, "I see what you mean"? (visual)

b) Does the person reply, "I hear what you're saying"? (auditory)

c) Does the person say something like "I could only understand how to use the new software program by sitting in the chair and clicking the mouse..."? (kinesthetic, or touch)

How to Enhance Rapport:

a) For a visual input person, emphasize the visual. "So I saw the character as someone like an eagle soaring over the valley."

b) For an auditory person, say something like, "You can hear the difference in the tone, can't you?"

c) For a kinesthetic person, "That went along smoothly, like gliding your hand across a polished marble table..."

Now it's your turn. Pick something you might say, then in your personal journal, note how you can modify such a phrase so that it enhances rapport with the three forms of input (visual, auditory, kinesthetic).

Points to Remember:

• **Darkest Secret #6: No matter what you have done for them, a Film or TV person will quickly write you off as "difficult," untrustworthy or "unprofessional"— if something rubs them the wrong way.**

• **Your Countermeasures:**

Be sure to prepare so you demonstrate comfort during your audition. Practice the methods to avoid these Audition Mistakes:

1) appearing negative

2) appearing needy

3) appearing arrogant

4) appearing unsure – like you lack confidence and seem to have nothing to offer

5) appearing unresponsive.

•

CHAPTER 7
DARKEST SECRET #7: YOU CAN LOSE AN ACTION MOVIE ROLE IN 10 SECONDS BECAUSE CASTING DECISION-MAKERS MAKE SNAP JUDGMENTS. AND IF THEY THINK YOU LACK BASIC SKILLS OF ACTING, THEY'LL FIND SOMEONE ELSE.

When you go into an audition, you need to show the director that you follow directions well. I have mentioned it elsewhere in this book, but it bears repeating. I directed two people to demonstrate their abilities to kick. I told them both to stay at opposite sides of the room. One actress began to show off and "try too hard." She put her partner in danger by kicking too close to him. We necessarily crossed her off the list. She lost the part in 10 seconds.

Recently, when you're going into auditions, the director often is a "tech-director." That is, they do not have formal acting training; their skills lie with special effects.

You need to "direct yourself" in that situation.

Your Countermeasures: Practice "directing yourself" in the face of vague, ambiguous direction.

Here are six methods for "directing yourself."

Method #1: Translate a Tech-director's "give me less" into "down the verb."

When a tech-director says, "Give me less," reduce the intensity of the verb of your objective. Observe the reduction in intensity of these verbs (in context):

a) I want to BRAINWASH him.

b) I want to persuade him.

Method #2: Translate Tech-director's "I like how you move your hand…" into thoughts of the character.

When an actor only focuses on a physical direction, she falls vulnerable to becoming shallow in a performance. She merely focuses on her hand. The solution is to find the thoughts that make the physical action come organically from the truth of the scene. For example, she can create a back-story like: my character moves her hand that way because it was crushed a bit when she was a little girl.

Another technique is to superimpose the thoughts that are appropriate over the actual dialogue of the script. You write your thoughts over the lines on the script. Many top actors' scripts are covered with their personal notes.

Method #3: Play the contrast.

In one feature film I directed, one actor played the contrast. During the dialogue, this actor concentrated on untangling wires and mumbled an occasional "uh-huh." To play the scene directly would be to look in the eyes of the scene partner and hang on every word. It was more realistic and fun for the audience seeing the contrast of energy between the characters.

Another example is how one particular actor gave the speech, "All the world is a stage." Instead of saying this speech with a flourish, this actor chose (on stage) to

almost mumble it while eating a piece of chicken. This choice did not work for me as an audience member. However, I applaud the freshness of the choice.

Method #4: Translate results-direction of "I want the audience to feel sad here" into something you can play.

Results-direction is when the director wants a specific result in the audience to occur. You can notice that an unhelpful pattern can be: a) the director says, "I want the audience to cry here" and b) the actor says in her mind, "Now, how can I do that? Maybe I should make my voice quiver on this line or whisper here or have one tear fall down there." This is mechanical.

Uta Hagen, one of the most revered acting teachers ever, said, "It doesn't matter if you cry, it matters if the audience cries." She was talking about dropping a narrow concern of just focusing on one specific technique—crying.

The solution is to transform the results-direction into something you can play. You add thoughts to your performance. To show pain and confusion on your face, create the thoughts that your character is having like: "Oh, no. What will I do?" or "Don't leave me," or "I'm so lost."

Method #5: Concentrate more on your scene partner; really listen.

Henry Fonda, considered one of greatest actors who

appeared in over 80 films, said, "Acting is reacting." To make your acting real and believable really watch and listen to your scene partner. The character you are portraying wants something specific. Perhaps the character wants to see a smile on the face of the other person. As the character, look for the desired response—even if as the actor you know that the script goes in the opposite direction. Henry Fonda pointed out that an actor must let go of certain script-knowledge in the moment of acting. His example was about a good actor portraying a cowboy, playing cards at 11:30 a.m. When the script calls for the cowboy to be shot at 12 noon, the good actor remembers that the character, while playing cards, has no idea about the script's outcome. Be real in the moment.

Method #6: Have a monologue (don't have a "loser's limp").

Often, I ask actors, "Do you have a monologue?" Frequently, I hear replies like:

"Um…uh…since I've moved to L.A., I'm not asked for a monologue much." Why disable yourself? Practicing your monologue is a way to keep up your acting skills. As a director, I ask for a monologue and I am really saying, "Here, show me your acting skills. Yes, I'm willing to devote some of my time to seeing you in action."

Have a monologue always ready (even if it's only 30 seconds long). In sports, there is the situation called "a loser's limp." A football player is hit, and then this particular person gets up and limps off the field—although he is not really hurt. He wants himself and the audience to feel, "Oh, isn't that too bad. Well, it's understandable that he won't play well for the rest of the game – he's hurt." To not have a monologue is to disable yourself. Instead, do everything to prepare yourself. Courage is easier when you're prepared.

Your Countermeasure: Make sure that you keep your acting skills fresh and ready to go.

Acting Essentials

This is a brief overview of acting essentials. As an acting coach, I help actors improve their performances through using skills and techniques.

1. Avoid over-thinking.

The best acting teachers point out that acting is not just saying lines. It is taking action. It is connecting with your partner and reacting to the person. "All good acting comes from the heart and there is no mentality about it," said Sandy Meisner, the master teacher who taught director Sydney Pollack (*Tootsie, Out of Africa*). Sandy used a technique called the Word Repetition Game in which new actors would repeat lines back and forth until the words were less important than learning to respond to your partner and your internal impulses.

2. Use preparation.

Some weak actors start a scene with no honest emotion. Then, possibly, they flow in and out of an emotion. Sandy Meisner said that the text is a canoe on a river of emotion. He emphasized, "Don't come in empty." Sandy continued, "The purpose of preparation is simple: it has to do with self-stimulation." He concluded, "Preparation is a kind of daydreaming." The idea is to choose something that changes you. It must be something personal. The character may be thrilled with a one dollar raise in the 1940's, and the actor may need to press her own button of daydreaming that her boyfriend just asked her to marry him. Sandy Meisner described the ideal situation: "The partner enters the room with a full emotion, and the two of them react to each other moment to moment." Sandy further clarified that preparation is "ambition or sex." He emphasized that these facets are sources of the actor's energy. The character may be elated over winning a job, and the actor's deeply personal preparation may be elation over a sexual conquest.

3. Be specific.

Actors often carefully observe someone in real life to develop a fleshed out character. They carefully choose specific behaviors. For example, for James Cameron's film *Avatar,* Sigourney Weaver confirmed that she played a James Cameron persona for her character. She said, "I teased him because to me I'm playing Jim Cameron in the movie as this kind of brilliant, approach-driven, idealistic perfectionist. But that same somebody has a great heart underneath. So I have to say I was always kind of channeling him."

4. Create fullness of emotion.

Do what is necessary to have full emotion when you begin a scene. George Henry Lewes, in *On Actors and the Art of Acting,* noted: "Macready, it is said, used to spend some minutes behind the scenes, lashing himself into an imaginative rage by cursing soto voce, and shaking violently a ladder fixed against the wall....He had worked himself up to the proper pitch of excitement which would enable him to express the rage of Shylock."

4. Flow with being nervous.

Fanny Brice, a comedian who rose to the top, always felt nervous before the first laugh. Her hands would tremble.

Sandy Meisner said, "So you're going to be nervous. Be nervous." An important point is to let go of the false idea that the goal is to be free of 'butterflies in the stomach.' Use the energy. Use it for preparation.

5. Make the part your own.

Sandy Meisner said that the process of making the part your own is filling up the cold text with your life. This is why Sandy did not limit his focus to emotional memory. Sandy felt that our in-the-moment response to our memories change. We need to keep alert to making powerful choices that move us. Sandy talked about a process of a) learning the lines with no emotion attached, b) do it in your own words, c) go through the script as written, and d) go back to the free improvisation.

I learned this process about make the part your own early in my training as an actor. I was called to play the part of a callous friend who abandons his friend "Tom" in the play *Tea and Sympathy*. The way I played the part, I expressed a deep feeling of shame that my character was leaving his friend in the lurch. Feeling conflicted came through my voice. One young actress came up to me at the end of my performance and said, "I felt more sorry for you than the other guy!" Wow! I had expressed the anguish I found in the part.

But later, when I directed the same scene with another actor "George," he had a whole different take. His portrayal was cold, as if the character "Tom" had put him in this bad position. His final word, "Sorry" was cold and cruel. And then the audience's sympathy all went to the character "Tom." During rehearsal, when I saw George's choices, I stood back. I did not try to impose my previous actor's choice. The performance of the play was different and really good!

6. Use "The Magic If"

To use "The Magic If" is to stimulate your own emotion using your imagination. Sandy Meisner used this example: "This scene is 'as if' you've just come from the funeral of your three-year-old brother." Sandy's technique went beyond 'emotional memory' because the memory or related emotion can change. He guided actors to make a choice that energizes them now and in this moment.

7. Find a substitution.

To use a substitution is to make a choice to stimulate your emotion with something that uniquely works for you. The character may be devastated about losing a job, and the actor may only feel devastated by losing a loved one. The actor uses an appropriate substitution. For example, for his *E.T.: The Extra-Terrestrial* audition, child actor Henry Thomas thought of the day his dog died. Henry cried. Director Steven Spielberg cried and hired Henry on the spot!

8. Make your technique personal and private

Sandy Meisner emphasized, "I'm talking about the personal, secret, intimate knowledge of preparation. So if somebody says to you, 'Where do you get that marvelous emotion you bring on in the third act?' The answer is simple: 'Talent.'" The point is to make a choice that deeply and uniquely moves you. For example, it is often considered unsophisticated and embarrassing to envy your friend. However, Kate White in her book, *9 Secrets of Women Who Get What They Want,* points out the power of envy to show us what we TRULY want. A number of successful women have used envy to spur their greatest efforts. The effective actor uses anything deeply personal: envy, jealousy, rage or fear.

9. Avoid indicating.

Indicating is to point to how a scene should be in a general way. The weak actor looks at the scene, "Oh, I should be angry here." Then, the weak actor, without full emotion, talks loud and knocks a chair over. The weak actor is showing or indicating what anger looks like. Instead, a powerful actor works from her personal specific choice. She chooses a personal substitution. The powerful actor then comes in the room and talks quietly, but the emotion is present. The audience is on the edge of their seats because they feel that the character can explode at any moment.

Some lines are repeated so often from feature film to feature film, that the actor needs to come up with something to make the line real and in the moment. For example, the line "have a bad feeling about this" is in the following *STAR WARS* Series films and expressed by the following characters: Obi Wan (*Episode I*), Anakin (*Episode II*), Obi Wan (*Episode III*), Luke (*Episode IV*), Han [portrayed by Harrison Ford] (*Episode IV*), Leia (*Episode V*), C3-PO (*Episode VI*).

And "have a bad feeling about this" is spoken by Harrison Ford again as Indiana Jones in *Indiana Jones and the Kingdom of the Crystal Skull*. Considering how the film was received, perhaps director Steven Spielberg had a bad feeling about this.

Another line that comes up in films a lot: "Let's go!"

10. Use an independent activity

As part of his training process, Sandy Meisner had actors use an independent activity. Before a scene or exercise would begin, one partner would be concentrating on some specific action: for example, writing an important letter to a parent. The other partner can enter the room, be in full emotion, and be straightening things out in the room. The independent activity of each actor can bring texture and realism to the scene. The second character may walk in, and her coping mechanism to distress is to fix or control her environment—that is revealed in her room-fixing activity.

The above has been a brief overview of acting essentials.

Remember, the director is looking for an actor who truly knows her craft. If any of the above methods are unclear to you, you now have homework. Study books and with an acting coach to get these methods clear in your mind—and at your fingertips. This is what is meant by "having the craft of acting."

Points to Remember:

• **Darkest Secret #7: You can lose an action movie role in 10 seconds because casting decision-makers make snap judgments. And if they think you lack basic skills of acting, they'll find someone else.**

• **Your Countermeasures:**

Be sure to study the basic skills of acting and rehearse every week. At least, rehearse your monologue a couple of times each week so that you're already ready to give an impromptu audition. Use these acting methods:

1. Avoid over-thinking.
2. Use preparation ("Don't come in empty").
3. Be specific.
4. Create fullness of emotion.
4. Flow with being nervous.

5. Make the part your own.
6. Use the "The Magic If."
7. Find a substitution.
8. Make your technique personal and private.
9. Avoid Indicating.
10. Use an independent activity.

•

CHAPTER 8
DARKEST SECRET #8: AN AGENT IS SUPPOSED TO GET YOU JOBS, BUT YOU MUST BE YOUR OWN BEST PROMOTER (A SELF-PROMOTER).

To get an agent (and to get roles) you need to demonstrate your value. But there is another element. You need to reach out to casting decision-makers. Here is an analogy. If you wanted to "bag a moose," you would need to go where the moose are. So the actor needs to go where casting decision-makers are (for example, industry events). This is part of the process of self-promotion. You learn how to approach people who can hire you.

We'll cover the S.E.L.F.P.R.O.M.O. process:

S – Structure your days.
E – Ease into conversations.
L – Learn about the other person.
F – Flow with challenges.

P – Prepare yourself.
R – Reveal the value you offer.
O – Offer your help.
M – Move the listener.
O – Out do the usual ways of promotion.

1. Structure your days.

Every day you need to accomplish something to promote yourself. During my workshops, I emphasize: "Keep score and achieve more." To get parts, to get an agent, to work with casting directors, you need to do a number of tasks in a systematic and consistent manner. That is, you need to plan every week to attend industry events, place the business cards' contact information into your contact management software program, send out postcards, make follow-up calls, attend workshops, and more.

You could note the activities on what I call a Self-Leadership Chart™. It is a grid that shows Mon, Tues, Wed, Thurs, Fri, Sat, Sun across the top. Then down the left side of the page you note tasks like these:

Check the Chart
Make phone calls to new contacts
Send postcards
Create a new promotional page
Go to networking event
Send follow-up email
Make follow-up calls
Make appointments
Interview casting decision-makers for my upcoming book
Find out about new clients for XYZ agency

2. Ease into conversations.

One easy way to start a conversation is to ask a gentle question like: "So how do you know Susan and Kevin?" I make the distinction of "gentle question" in that you're asking a question that is easy for the person to answer. Be careful to avoid sounding like an interrogator. In addition, a gentle question is not too personal so that you avoid creating an awkward moment.

3. Learn about the other person.

Before you call someone new, do your homework. For example, I once talked with a particular best-selling author, and he mentioned that he worked with a top sports agent.

"Oh, is that 'Joe'?" I asked.

"How do you know Joe?" the author inquired.

"I read every word of your book," I replied. Just before I called him, I also scanned through his book to refresh my memory.

4. Flow with challenges.

Prepare backup plans for errors you might make.

a) For conversational mistakes . . .

you can recover by using a phrase like: "That's not what I meant to say…I meant to say…" or "Oh, forgive me, I was just [excited, a bit tired…]"

b) For an error with an agent…

Here's an example of how one actress, "Sandra," smoothed things out with her agent. Her agent "Mira" forbids her actors to have any extra contact with her clients (advertising agencies). One time, Sandra sent a thank you note to one of Mira's clients. Sandra immediately sent an apology note to Mira for making an error. In addition to the note, some people send a small box of chocolates as a goodwill gesture.

5. Prepare yourself.

Best-selling author Harvey Mackay prepared for being interviewed by Larry King on the TV show CNN Larry King Live by using a number of techniques including:

a) Watch 18 episodes of Larry's interview show.

b) Read Larry's book.

c) Rehearse the interview process with a radio interviewer.

The interview went so well that Larry King invited Harvey to return to the program over five more times.

Now it's your turn. Read and study about the industry. Get training, including the skills to make a great first impression.

6. Reveal the value you offer.

One of the most vivid ways to demonstrate the value you offer is to tell a story (an anecdote). We are conditioned to tune into stories. How do you give a person the impression that you're reliable? You tell a story. You sprinkle the details about yourself into the conversation. Here is an example. An actress, Samantha, says: "It was great working with Director Janet Smythe on the feature film *One Rough Night*. I really appreciated it when she said, 'Samantha, you're an actress I can count on to really do your homework.'"

7. Offer your help.

You need to stand out from other actors. Casting decision-makers sometimes categorize actors as needy people who merely impinge on their time. Many casting decision-makers see actors as just selfish people wanting something from them.

How do you counteract this? You find some way to be helpful to casting decision-makers. For example, just today, I was called by an actress who had recommended me to a casting decision-maker for a role calling for a middle-aged Asian man (that's me). The actress is helping the casting decision-maker find what she's looking for. And if the role is a match, the actress has done me a favor, too. Best-selling author Zig Ziglar said, "You can have anything you want if you help enough other people get what they want."

Picture that each day you're planting seeds by helping people and connecting with people. When I teach clients and graduate students about networking, I emphasize the "3 words of networking: Help them first." It is important to ask people for what you want, but do not lead with your request. Remember: help them first.

8. Move the listener.

You move the listener with…

a) word pictures

b) phrases appealing to the senses

c) salting phrases

a) Use word pictures. A phrase I have heard is "Ask not the sparrow how the eagle flies." This is a visual image.

b) Use phrases appealing to the senses like: "You could hear a pin drop—the audience was so quiet and captivated."

c) Use *salting phrases*. You get someone interested in

listening to you by peaking the person's interest. Some people are reluctant to give full attention. It's almost like the old phrase "You can lead a horse to water but you can't make him drink." Author Steven K. Scott wrote, "You get that horse to drink by salting his oats first."

So your job is to get people to be "thirsty" to hear what you're going to say next. In effect, you drop little hints, similar to "salting oats."

Here are examples:

1) "When I was talking to best-selling author Marcia Wieder she had a strategy to ____. Would you like to hear about that?"

2) "Lynda Obst [producer of Sleepless in Seattle] talked about how she got her films financed. Would you like to hear her strategies?"

9. Take your self-promotion to a higher level.

The promotion elements most actors use are:

1. Headshot
2. Business cards (with headshot)
3. Resume
4. Postcard with headshot on it

These are bare minimum required elements. It's better that you reach to a higher level of self-promotion. Such elements can include:

a) Have videos on YouTube.com.
b) Have a website.
c) Consider producing and starring in your own

webisodes.

d) Consider being a speaker.

e) Use an electronic newsletter or Twitter (perhaps, a blog).

f) Place on your postcards photos of you on the set. (Create the impression: "Oh, this actor is always working.")

g) Find out how to help the agency (Ask, "Who is your ideal client?").

h) Write a book or article—and interview the key casting-decision-makers.

i) Consider being a stand-up comedian.

Method #A: Have videos on YouTube.com.

When someone tells me that he is an actor, I ask, "Do you have any videos on YouTube?"

Through YouTube.com, people now have the fastest way to demonstrate their acting abilities.

Now, it's your turn. Would you like to demonstrate your acting skills? You could set up a video camera on a tripod and record yourself performing a monologue. Here is a hint so that you can ensure the quality of your video clip: be sure to have a microphone near you. It is too painful to hear videos in which the viewer mostly hears the reverb of the room instead of the clear voice of the actor. For example, people in my office give up within 10 seconds if the audio is painful to listen to.

Method #B: Have a website.

Do you have a website? My colleagues sometimes talk about how we think someone is not serious enough about her craft of acting if she does not have a website. On your website place a demo video, your resume, your headshot and other photos. In addition, it could be helpful to post a photo of yourself on the set of a significant production with the star of whatever film or show you're in. It gives the impression that you're "always working."

Method #C: Consider producing and starring in your own webisodes

If you want to demonstrate that you're an ideal actor for romantic comedy roles, show us! How? Film three brief episodes of a webisodes series. Webisodes are short films that you place on YouTube.com and your own website. Show us through the webisodes that you have comedic timing if that's the kind of role you're interested in.

If you want to show that you're ideal for action movie roles, consider filming a 30-second commercial of an action movie. Make this an original movie idea. Who knows—you might even be able to sell the idea as the basis for a screenplay. Or if someone says, "Do you have a screenplay done of that movie?" you could say, "I'm revising a draft of the screenplay. I think I'll have a version available in about 32 days." You could write a draft, and Perhaps hire someone to help you revise it.

(More information about producing your own short film or feature film is in a later section of this book entitled: *BOOK II: Taking Control of Your Career: Producing Your Own Short Film, Feature Film or Web Series.*)

Method #D: Consider being a speaker.

A speaker is someone who conducts workshops or gives speeches in front of audiences.

Reasons to be a speaker:

1. Someone in the audience may be able to get you a role.
2. You will stand out.

3.You will show that you're a professional.
4. You can get on television and radio shows.
5. It makes it easier to get an agent.
6. You quickly expand your network.

Details about the benefits of being a speaker:

1. Someone in the audience may be able to get you a role.

Patrick Stewart (*Star Trek: The Next Generation*) won the role of Captain Jean-Luc Picard when he took part in a presentation attended by Bob Justman (Associate Producer of *Star Trek: The Next Generation*). Bob called *Star Trek* creator Gene Roddenberry and said, "Gene, I think we've found our captain."

2. You will stand out.

There are thousands of actors who only have acting training. But as a speaker, you will stand out in how you think on your feet. People notice that good speakers smoothly adlib and work with audiences.

3. You will show that you're a professional.

Agents are afraid of using new people because they occasionally run into 'flaky actors' who don't show up, who are late or who are demanding. A professional speaker cannot do anything flaky or they don't get work.

4. You can get on television and radio shows.

Television and radio shows tend to ignore actors just starting out. However, these shows have a steady diet of book authors who share methods for getting things done. The benefit of being on various radio and television shows is that it proves to a prospective agent that you're a live wire—

that you're going someplace. And by the way, you would be an ideal leading actor to promote a film on The Tonight Show or some other interview show.

5. It makes it easier to get an agent.

At one point, I found it easier to get someone to represent me. How? I called a particular agent and said, "I was a guest on a television show and one of your actors, Susan, mentioned your firm." Then I mentioned that I'm a national speaker. My credibility was

heightened. I met the agent at her office and soon she had me booked for a number of roles.

6. You quickly expand your network.

In the entertainment industry, it's all about contacts. The more people you know, the more opportunities you can be exposed to.

Choose a Topic to Speak On:

What topic(s) would be a match for you to speak on?

I know actors who speak on these topics:

1. Communication
2. Salespeople using acting techniques to perform at their best
3. Acing a job interview

Method #E: Use an electronic newsletter or Twitter (perhaps, a blog)

An e-newsletter (that is really an email message sent to list of e-subscribers) is a great way for you to be in contact with hundreds of people, perhaps once a month. Some people like to send out the e-newsletter more often, but recently many people tend to unsubscribe when they feel their in-box is being swamped with too many messages.

You remind them that you exist and that you're an actor. You must put useful tips or methods in the e-newsletter or it will be perceived as merely advertising, and people will unsubscribe as fast as an Indy 500 racecar. What would be relevant tips? For example, an e-newsletter entitled *Actors and Directors Success Secrets* would attract both actors and filmmakers. You can make the newsletter include relevant film and television industry news and techniques for the reader to fast forward her career. Some people find that using Twitter is a great way to stay in contact with Followers. If your Tweets include useful strategies and methods for people in the film industry, it's more likely that people will continue to follow your Tweets (or blog posts).

Method #F: Place on your postcards—photos of you on the set. (Create the impression: "Oh, this actor is always working.")

Let's face it. Many people do not like to read. And they don't appreciate "junk mail." A postcard with a handwritten note can work because it's brief and now with all of us using email and chatting online, a postcard is a bit rare.

You can make your postcard more compelling by including a photo of you on the set with a major star. For tips on how to get such a photo, we'll explore methods in the later section entitled *BOOK IV: Self-promotion and How to Do Well on Television and Radio (and When and How to Use Photos with Big Stars).*

Method #G: Find out how to help the agency (Ask, "Who is your ideal client?").

Make yourself stand out. Help people first. In any

networking situation, ask a gentle question like "How can I be supportive of what you're doing?" or "Who is your ideal client?" Then you can follow-up after you do a Google search (or look through your own contacts) for a possible client for the agency you wish to work for.

Method #H: Write a book or article—and interview the key casting decision-makers

Writing a book or article (or blog article) gives you access to thousands of people. Why? Because many people in Hollywood are savvy about the importance of self-promotion.

Your first thought may be: "I don't know how to interview anyone." Okay. Let's take a moment to look at possible questions you could use for interviewing a notable person:

1. What are the Do's?
2. What are the Don'ts?
3. What is an unusual way that worked for you?
4. What is an unusual way that failed when someone tried it with you?
5. What impresses you?
6. What turns you off?
7. Knowing what you know now, what would you have done differently?

So now you have an idea about what you could say when interviewing someone.

How can you get an interview with a Hollywood notable person? To start it off, you could leave a voicemail:

"I'm writing a book [article] entitled ______. The book would not be complete without you. We can do a phone interview for ten to fifteen minutes."

Accurately Quote People; Use a Recorded Phone Interview.

The way to accurately quote people is to use a telephone conversation recording system. For example, you could get a recording system from Amazon.com. (At the time of this writing one can get a unit on Amazon.com for $14.85).

How can you record an interview in an appropriate manner? Call the person, and ask to interview them for 10 minutes. Say that you need to phone back and engage your interview recording system. Say, "When I call you, I'll ask you if it is okay to record the interview." This is the way that you get the person's approval on the recording itself. By the way, use a timer. End on time. Hollywood people are busy, and they appreciate your professionalism.

Method I: Consider being a stand-up comedian.

There is a long list of stand-up comedians who made the transition to film and television. They gained the attention of casting personnel. Let's note the career paths of Jim Carrey, Tim Allen, Sarah Silverman, Roseanne, Chris Rock, Kevin James, Ray Romano, Whoopi Goldberg and many others. I recall working with a backup singer more than twenty years ago. Then about three years ago, I was flipping through cable channels and saw her doing some stand-up comedy.

A side note: Improve the self-promotion power of your business cards.

Many actor business cards only have a photo and contact information. Stand out from the rest. Out do those cards. Add a couple of credits to your business card.

Here is an example:

Joe Smith, Actor

David (lead) in *Red House* feature film

Joey (lead) in *No Bricks* feature film

* * * * * *

Work a Lot by Getting Passionate about Self-Promotion. Get connected with the value that an actor provides.

An actor provides a service to other people. How? Notice how the actor…

a) inspires

b) teaches

c) shows activities to avoid

d) shows the consequences of ill-advised actions

e) helps people treasure their loved ones

Now, aren't you excited about being an actor? It is a noble profession. Many of us, deep in our hearts, want to make a contribution to other people. In fact, a spiritual text emphasizes, "I am here only to be truly helpful." I encourage you to get excited about the value you provide as an actor. In addition, realize that part of your job is to self-promote so you can work as an actor.

A powerful phrase is "Doing well by doing good." Connect with the goodness you provide. Just imagine that part of your art IS self-promotion. You are an actor. You want to perform—to enrich people's lives—and your own life. That is the Divine within you calling out. In additional, there is an important part for you to play, a great self-promoter. This role is actually your best self—that is a confident, clear communicator, who creates rapport with people easily. To help you fulfill that role, here are the *Great Actor's 3 Traits:* Energy, Truth, and Audience-Focus.

ENERGY: Energy for self-promotion actually comes from

your inner child, which is the part of you that whispers I want this. We want to make that whisper into a roar that gets you moving. It's the roar of desire that has me writing this book at 3:05 a.m. on a day off during the holiday season. I want to help you make your dreams come true.

We need you to have the energy to...

1. Make lists of contacts.
2. Use a contact management database (a software program that helps you track your interactions with hundreds or thousands of people).
3. Use a calendar for following up with people. For follow-up, a calendar is important because you do not want to push too hard by sending too many emails or postcards – or placing too many phone calls within a short time period.

TRUTH: We are focused on your Best Self: the confident you that gracefully walks up to new people at a networking event. In addition, when you're acting during your audition, you want to connect with the truth of you as the character.

AUDIENCE-FOCUS: Your audience includes casting decision-makers. So what does the Agent, Casting Director, Producer or Director want to know about you?

1. You're good.
2. You're reliable.
3. You're pleasant to work with.
4. Other people think good things about you and want to hire you again and again.
5. You have previous credits and experience.
6. Your personal traits match the role.
7. You're good in interviews with the media.

If you have not interacted with film industry personnel, let's talk about characteristics of film industry people:

1. Busy
2. Jaded
3. Some push others around
4. Some are cold

How do you effectively respond to negative traits of industry people?

1. Person is busy: you're brief.

2. Person is jaded: you're professional in your style and you avoid novice mistakes (which we note in this book).

3. Person pushes others around: you maintain your calm.

5. Person is cold: you direct your own thoughts with empowering phrases like: "Oh, she doesn't know me yet. When she knows me, she'll know that I bring value."

Now that you know some effective ways to respond, you can rehearse, improve your skills, promote yourself and gain more roles.

Crucial Key Elements of Self-Promotion for Actors

Here are the key elements of self-promotion for actors.

1. Follow-up is vital.
2. Be the invited guest (gentle touches).
3. Stand out from the crowd.
4. Make your first credits happen.

1. Follow-up is vital.

Researchers demonstrate that people often need to be contacted (or asked to buy) five times before they say, "yes." Unfortunately, novice actors often think: "All it takes is that they'll see my headshot and know that I'm perfect for the role." Instead, like a professional salesperson, you need to tastefully follow-up. Follow-up can be via a postcard, email message or phone call.

2. Be the invited guest (gentle touches).

Marketing expert and best-selling author Dan Kennedy emphasizes the idea of being an invited guest. How can you do that? One way is to focus on your follow-up efforts as a way to lead with helpful information for the casting decision-maker. Then you have separated yourself from a casting person's idea of "a selfish actor begging for a part." Instead, you are a kind professional helping a colleague. What could be helpful information? Here's an example. Some casting agencies cast for personnel for corporations' promotional events. If you can help such a casting agency gain a new client, you certainly stand out. How? You keep track of all types of contacts. Monitor what kind of promotional events are happening. Learn about opportunities. And you become a "connector"—that is, you help people by connecting them to others who can help them accomplish their objectives.

3. Stand out from the crowd.

How do people tend to remember a particular detail? Research shows that a difference makes something memorable. For example, one casting director said she remembers one actress as "the actress who wrote a book on knitting." Another example: "Oh yeah, he's the actor who is a national speaker."

4. Make your first credits happen.

In the following chapters, I cover numerous details about how you can take a proactive role and even produce short projects to ensure you have your first credits and film/video experience. To get work, your resume needs to show that you have worked! It feels like a Catch-22. The later section entitled *BOOK II: Taking Control of Your Career: Producing Your Own Short Film, Feature Film or Web Series* is helpful.

* * * * * *

Key Steps to Get an Agent

1. Have the usual materials ready and with top quality.

Usual materials are your headshot and a resume. A demo video is also often requested.

A headshot is a photograph used by actors and actresses to gain roles. Traditionally, the headshot was distributed as an 8 x 10 print of the performer in which the face is clearly shown. The name of the actor is usually printed on the bottom right hand corner of the image. Traditionally, the resume was stapled to the back of the 8 x 10 print.

Currently, many casting decision-makers prefer using email and attachments. They often request that you send, via email, a link to a demo video and/or attach your headshot and resume to an email message.

Improve the Quality of Your Headshot:

1. Have light reflected in your eyes to make them sparkle. Avoid too much glowing. Recently I saw a headshot in which the eyes glowed like the actor was a science fiction alien character. That's too much.

2. Have the background darker than your skin tone. Watch out that your hair doesn't fade into the background. Request that the photographer use a hairlight. (Most photographers will do that as a standard procedure.)

Improve the Quality of Your Resume:

1. Include the standard information: your height, weight, hair color, eye color, and training. Include your experience in film, television, commercials, and print.
2. For training, you may want to show your breadth of experience in acting, stage combat, commercials and/or modeling.
3. For special skills, include what makes you stand out. For example, one actor includes "public speaker, improvisation, stand-up humor, martial arts, stage combat, guitar, piano."

* * * * * *

Method #2: Have some first credits.

In later sections of this book, I reveal numerous ways to have your first credits—and not merely to wait for someone to "give you permission" to act. You can produce a short film with your friends and have an instant credit. For print work, you can also write an article for a friend's electronic newsletter. Attach your headshot and then you can have a credit like:

Print
Movers and Shakers Monthly

Method #3: Call the agent's office and ask what the process is.

Perhaps a particular agent only sees new talent once on a month on the third Tuesday between 2:00 p.m. and 4:30 p.m. Another agent might say, "Send in five headshots. We'll get back to you if appropriate."

Method #4: Submit to all the agents in your area.

Follow their preferred procedure to the letter! You must precisely follow directions. You're making a first impression here. Here are examples of idiosyncratic preferences that agents/casting directors have:

- One agent prefers a resume to be glued to the back of a headshot (this is unusual).
- One agent prefers headshots that have a second image (small) in the bottom right corner (this is unusual).
- One casting director specifically says, "Only give me four headshots." Do NOT send her more!
- One casting director says, "Don't send me printed headshots. I do everything via email now."

Method #5: Get a referral.

The way I connected with an agent was through a referral. I was on a television show with another actor. She mentioned her agent. Since I had developed a relationship with her, she kindly gave me a referral to her agent, "Mira." I called Mira and was granted a meeting. Within days, Mira invited me to work with her and go to auditions that she had set up.

Method #6: Participate in showcases.

Casting directors and agents attend showcases to seek new talent. Another event that helps actors is a staged reading. I held a staged reading and three of the actors gained roles in one of my feature films. In addition, a number of actors I know have participated in showcases and were singled out for representation by agents.

* * * * * *

Key Steps to Work with Casting Directors

1. Register with a number of casting directors.

First ask your fellow actors if the casting director has cast anyone they know. Some casting directors are busy and others are not. A number of casting directors charge a onetime fee to register with them. If you choose a busy casting director, your registration is only the beginning of the story. Casting directors have literally thousands of people in their files. You must stay in contact with casting directors and your postcard can help in that, often, your postcard will cross their desk just when they need someone of your type.

2. Help the casting director.

Stay in touch. Ask, "How can I be supportive of what you're doing?" Perhaps she is looking for a short person to portray a cartoon character. You'll make points if you find one for her.

3. Consider being an intern.

What does an intern do? Often, the intern is the person who calls a number of actors to see if they are available on a particular day for filming. An intern also answers the phone and screens calls.

4. Call and send a postcard.

After you establish a relationship with a casting director, then send a postcard to stay in touch. Occasionally telephone the casting director. Remember to not expect a return call from a casting director. Casting directors state that they're too busy to return calls to actors.

5. Create a you can count on me impression.

Always be early for any filming session. Make sure that the casting director feels she can count on you. If an actor is late or fails to show up, it causes trouble for the casting director. Casting directors have clients like agencies do. For example, one casting director I know does bookings all over the country for Nintendo and their casting needs. Actors are needed to portray certain characters for promotional events.

* * * * * *

Key Steps to Get Parts on Your Own

1. Meet producers and directors in other settings

When a producer or director is holding a workshop or book signing—go! For example, I often cast roles in my projects (and refer actors for other projects) from students in my classes because I know these people and what they can do. Attend screenings. In other sections of this book, you'll find strategies for networking at events.

2. Hang out, be an intern or work at an industry office.

You might consider being an intern at a casting director's office. As a film director, I visited a casting director who is a friend. Another feature film director walked in, and I asked about his upcoming projects. He told me about his upcoming film, a retelling of the Romeo and Juliet story in an urban setting. To get him to consider me for a part, I asked the other director, "Do you need an Asian American teacher (since I am an Asian American actor)?" I didn't get a role, but I did serve as a fight scene consultant on that feature film.

My point is that you need to be at the right place at the right time to get casting decision-makers to consider you for a role.

3. Become known or a celebrity

If one is a celebrity who demonstrates poise, one may find the casting decision-makers offer roles. Even celebrities like Anthony Robbins and Dr. Phil McGraw have performed roles in feature films. This book provides, in the section *Self-promotion and How to Do Well on Television and Radio,* material on how to perform effectively as a television guest.

4. Work behind the scenes on productions

Do someone a favor, and in many cases, the person is inclined to do a favor for you. When you work behind the scenes (especially on an independent feature film), you're helping the director, and she feels favorably toward you. Often, because you're on the set, you're in the right place for a spontaneous opportunity to act. For example, one of my editors told me of her friend who had a large van to haul filmmaking equipment; he got roles in independent feature films.

5. Use a contact management program and stay in touch.

You need to remind casting decision-makers that you're still in the business and that you're working. Use a contact management program to keep notes about the last time you sent a postcard or made a call to a particular decision-maker. Use a calendar to also remind yourself to consistently touch base with casting decision-makers. By the way, make sure that you call people and take an interest in their lives. When appropriate, you can ask, "How are things going?" Later in the conversation, you can ask, "How can I be supportive of what you're doing?"

6. Use the Internet.

Go to Google.com and other search engines and type in keywords like "acting" "casting" and others. I have personally seen this process work. For one film in which I portrayed the lead villain, other actors submitted their headshot via the Internet.

7. Use Email.

A key way to stay in contact with people is sending brief email messages. When you contact casting decision-makers, send an email message that provide useful information. What would a producer or director want to know? You could send a list of film festivals, financing contacts, and distribution contacts.

Develop your industry contacts. Some time ago, I auditioned for two producers and learned that they needed a makeup person. I called a casting director and another producer to find a good makeup person. Then, I emailed (with the makeup person's permission) her phone number to the producers. The last I heard, she had a good chance to get the work. Then I will have helped all three people involved by my facilitating the connection.

If you auditioned for a particular role, you can send brief email messages like: "I'm still excited about the role of Joe" or "Every week I have three martial arts lessons, so I'm ready for the part of Mark."

8. Consider Backstage.com.

I know actors who sing the praises of Backstage.com.

The website describes itself with: "Founded in 1960, Back Stage is the world's most trusted name in casting, auditions, and entertainment-industry opportunities. Back Stage helps actors, models, dancers, singers, comedians, variety performers, voice-over artists, and crew members find gigs—while helping casting directors, producers, directors, choreographers, photographers, writers, agents, and other entertainment-industry employers find amazing talent for all of their projects."

Backstage.com provides resources for actors on both U.S. coasts. You click on either the "LA Actor" link or "NY Actor" link. The resources include articles, columns, a blog, notices for classes and notices for roles in productions. You can post your headshot and resume for consideration by casting personnel. For current fees and to see if you feel that the website is valuable to you, you'll need to view the appropriate pages of the website.

Points to Remember:

- **Darkest Secret #8: An agent is supposed to get you jobs, but YOU must be your own best promoter (a self-promoter).**

- **Your Countermeasure:**

Consider doing more than average efforts on self-promotion including:

a) Have videos on YouTube.com.

b) Have a website.

c) Consider producing and starring in your own webisodes.

d) Consider being a speaker.

e) Use an electronic newsletter or Twitter.

f) Place on your postcards photos of you on the set (create the impression: "Oh, this actor is always working").

g) Find out how to help an agency (Ask, "Who is your ideal client?")

h) Write a book or article—and interview the key casting-decision-makers.

i) Consider being a stand-up comedian.

CHAPTER 9
DARKEST SECRET #9: PEOPLE WILL LIE TO YOUR FACE DAILY AND NOT CARE BECAUSE "THAT'S HOW HOLLYWOOD BUSINESS IS DONE."

The Hollywood people don't like to say "no." Why? Because people don't like to hear "no"—it hurts. And people take offense. Hollywood people seek to avoid making too many enemies because they may be forced to work with someone later in their career. Along these lines, Walter Winchell said, "Be nice to those you meet on the way up because you will meet them on the way down."

So if you ask for a simple answer to "Did they cast me?" you're likely to hear something vague like "They're still considering a number of options."

You may not hear that you lost a role until there's an announcement online or through an industry periodical that someone else got the part. And even if you gained the role, you may lose it. For example, Julia Ormond was originally cast as Superman's Kryptonian mother (in *Man of Steel*, directed by Zack Snyder), but she lost her role to Ayelet Zurer.

In addition to casting upset, Hollywood is the site of many forms of maneuvering in deal making. For example, James Cameron manipulated negotiations to find a way to get Sigourney Weaver to portray "Ripley" in *Aliens.* Cameron telephoned Arnold Schwarzenegger's agent for an informal chat and mentioned that thanks to his newfound standing in Hollywood following The Terminator, he had decided "to make this film entirely his own by writing Ripley out." According to Cameron's plan, Schwarzenegger's agent immediately relayed the information to his colleague representing Weaver at ICM. This agent called 20th Century-Fox Head of Production Lawrence Gordon and the two men decided to guard against Ripley being written out. They got Weaver's deal completed fast.

Kirk Douglas infamously used manipulation when he wanted to hire various top level stars (Peter Ustinov, Laurence Olivier, Charles Laughton) for his production of *Spartacus.* To get so many big stars to take on supporting roles, Kirk Douglas showed each a different script in which their character was emphasized.

So what can you do with this knowledge that you may be lied to or kept out of the loop?

Your Countermeasure to the lies and manipulations in Hollywood: Think through how you might be hurt. Decide what your priorities are and make backup plans.

For example, you may decide to take a role in an independent film, and the film's producer promised deferred salaries (you get paid when the film makes money).

Unfortunately, there are "bottom feeder" distributors who never pay the filmmakers. So you don't get a salary. But you might be seen in such a film. For example, Joe Pesci was in a low budget crime film *The Death Collector,* but he gave up on acting and was managing a restaurant. Then he got a phone call inviting him to talk with Robert DeNiro. He returned the phone call expecting that it was a friend pulling a prank on him. It was Robert DeNiro wanting to talk with Joe about the role of Robert's "brother" in *Raging Bull,* directed by Martin Scorsese.

My point is, that if you think through how you might be hurt, you can set up backup plans. Here's a backup plan: if you can, you might keep a job earning rent money and see if a local independent film could schedule your scenes for the weekends. So if you never see a dime directly from the film, you didn't lose your steady income.

At the beginning of a career, many actors realize that their way to improve their craft of film acting requires that they work (paid or unpaid) on some film sets. So if, in the beginning, you don't make much money, you can decide it's okay. Why? Because you're still living your life as a performing actor. It's a matter of your personal priorities.

Points to Remember:

- **Darkest Secret #9: People will lie to your face daily and not care because "that's how Hollywood business is done"**

- **Your Countermeasure:**

When you consider that you may be lied to or kept out of the loop, think through how you might be hurt. Decide what your priorities are and make backup plans.

CHAPTER 10
DARKEST SECRET #10: A MULTI-MILLION DOLLAR FILM THAT EARNS MILLIONS OF DOLLARS WILL STILL (ACCORDING TO "CREATIVE ACCOUNTING") SHOW NO PROFITS. AN INDEPENDENT FILM MAY NOT EARN ANY MONEY. SO YOU BETTER MAKE GOOD DECISIONS BASED ON MORE THAN A PROMISED DEFERRED PAYCHECK.

It's reported that Sean Connery (originator of the James Bond role) found it necessary to sue a number of studios he worked for. Why? He had been promised a share of profits but certain studios were not paying him according to the signed agreement.

As a side note: I was at a Hollywood party and one of the revelers talked about how his friend, a makeup artist, had a rough time trying to conceal Sean's many tattoos.

A few years ago, I ran an audition and learned of one actor's temporary solution to having an acting career and still paying living expenses. He was making a living as a computer special effects team member and he was also starring in a few modest budget direct-to-video feature films. Somehow, he was able to make a comfortable living and still pursue his film acting dreams. It sounds good to me.

When an actor starts doing well, perhaps he or she wants to put some money aside for legal expenses instead of tossing too much money aside in frivolous pursuits. What legal expenses? As mentioned, Sean Connery had to sue certain studios to get his due payments. As actors become well-known, some must defend themselves from frivolous lawsuits.

At the beginning of your career be careful about getting a reputation for "pushes back too much." That is, it is dangerous for you to be considered "trouble" to film production companies. But it is also "okay" to be a person who ensures that they are treated fairly. Only you can decide if it is in your best interest to pursue legal action—on a case-by-case basis. If you do not know what your best course of action is, you may want to hire an entertainment attorney for one hour only. Be sure to write out your questions before your appointment, and check off the questions as you go through them with the attorney.

Dustin Hoffman talked about how he put money aside during the tough early days of his acting career. He had a collection of glass jars marked "rent," "food" and "entertainment." He made sure to save money (in the jars) to keep himself alive between acting gigs.

My point is that since you may be in some films that "make no money," you must be careful with the money you earn as immediate payment. You can make good decisions and decide to take certain roles for reasons like: a) the sheer joy to act in a production with good writing or b) the role demonstrates your range and can lead to other roles in other productions.

Points to Remember:

- **Darkest Secret #10: A multi-million dollar film that earns millions of dollars will still (according to "creative accounting") show no profits. An independent film may not earn any money. So you better make good decisions based on more than a promised deferred paycheck.**

- **Your Countermeasure:**

Since you may be in some films that "make no money," you must be careful with the money you earn as immediate payment. Have a budget and follow it. Think through the decision to take a particular role. Pay attention to your intuition. Perhaps you'll decide to take a role for reasons like: a) the sheer joy to act in a production with good writing or b) the role demonstrates your range and can lead to other roles in other productions.

•

CHAPTER 11
DARKEST SECRET #11: NOBODY CARES ABOUT YOU. YOU'RE MERELY A COG IN THEIR FILMMAKING MACHINE. YOU NEED TO MAKE YOURSELF STRONG PHYSICALLY, EMOTIONALLY AND SPIRITUALLY. (YOU'RE EXPECTED TO BE TOUGH.)

How do you get tough? You exercise, sleep well and enjoy excellent nutrition.

For *Terminator II: Judgment Day,* Robert Patrick portrayed the T-1000, the physically superior android to the one portrayed by Arnold Schwarzenegger. Robert began training with Steve Cook, a martial arts master. Robert said to an interviewer, "I did this on my own, as character development. I learned how to control my body, how to stretch it out to make it look fluid. I even changed my breathing. Steve suggested that I go through all of my workouts breathing through my nose. I found that breathing through my nose evenly—even while running very fast—helped to create a machinelike quality in the T-1000."

Robert also trained with commando trainer Uzi Gal. Robert said, "We did weightlifting, strengthening my legs so that I'd be able to sprint very fast and run without fatigue after a lot of takes. It was very military and very tough. The first day I worked out with Uzi I didn't know if I was going to get through it. We worked from about five o'clock in the morning, three or four workouts a day, everyday for nine weeks. It actually changed my lifestyle some. I quit smoking for one thing. It also helped me to grow as a person and to focus on the character. When you go into a role like this, you've got to go full throttle."

For *Terminator II*, Linda Hamilton also trained with a personal trainer for four months. She said, "[I worked out] six mornings a week, two to three hours a day. I lifted weights and did a lot of aerobic conditioning. It was wonderful to see myself transformed. I had muscles, and I was a hundred times stronger than I had ever been, which was a good thing because I would never have made it through the film otherwise. I was battered and chased and slammed into walls and everything else. Every day was a physical challenge; but because of the training, I was prepared for it. I was as much of an Arnold Schwarzenegger as I could be."

Linda trained with Uzi Gal and learned how to handle weapons and hand-to-hand combat techniques. She said, "I did that for two months, and they were the longest two months of my life. It was grueling. I could have stopped at any time, but I didn't because I knew that this was the process Sarah [her character] had gone through. It had beaten her down and made her old and wise and strong, and I had to understand all of that before I could do the role. So even though it was very, very hard, the training helped me to focus on Sarah and understand her. She doesn't have room in her life for an expression or a smile. She's all business, because in this kind of combat there is no place for emotion. If your weapon jams, you don't get mad, you fix it —or you die."

The producers and director of *Deep Blue Sea* had seen Thomas Jane in a number of well-received independent features and invited him to portray shark wrangler Carter Blake. Thomas said, "I knew it was going to be tough and challenging and worth every second. You get 4,000 gallons of water dumped on you. You get dragged around by an 8,000-pound shark. Fall off of ladders. Get burned. Drowned. Beaten. It's been fun."

Thomas emphasized, "When you read the script it says, 'Carter steps outside.' It doesn't say, 'Carter steps outside and gets hit by 4,000 gallons of water, and a helicopter hovers over his head in a swirling tropical thunderstorm at sea, and suddenly a two-ton shark just misses him by inches.' But that's what it's like working on a [Director Renny] Harlin picture."

The actor prepared for the role with an extensive workout regimen. He admitted, "Sometimes even that didn't ready me for the work; but it's been a great ride." The vital point here is: when you want to do action roles, be sure to exercise consistently!

What the Director is Thinking (about the actor's fitness level)

The first indication of your fitness level that a director encounters is your list of abilities on your resume like: "jogging, weightlifting, skateboarding, horseback riding." Go the next step and be prepared. Put together a 'composite card.' That is, have a card with, perhaps four photos of you in action. Demonstrate that you're fit and have done action scenes. I receive 'composite cards' from actors and stunt people.

When you demonstrate that you're fit, you demonstrate that you're versatile. Jackie Chan (*Rush Hour*) is known for his martial arts skills in fight scenes. However, the Jackie Chan Fan Club USA reports that Jackie does not practice martial arts every day. The Fan Club reports, "He usually jogs and does a workout with light weights."

So I'm emphasizing that consistent exercise is important. Do check with your doctor about what is appropriate for your current fitness level.

Key #1: Use an easy system.

My clients use a *Self-Leadership Chart*. On the chart, you note Monday through Sunday. Down the left margin you note various exercise elements like: bicycling, jogging, weight training, abdomen exercises, stationary bicycle. You place a star or check mark for each exercise ritual you accomplish on a given day. Decide also on how you'll reward yourself (what I call a "self-reward"). Perhaps exercising two days in a row leads to a self-reward of going to the movie theater or seeing a home video. You'll find how you can motivate yourself.

Key #2: Use interesting variety.

Rebecca varies her exercises from day-to-day, which makes them more interesting to her. Monday through Thursday, she selects one of these: 1) exercise video, 2) walk, 3) run, or 4) stationary bicycle. On Fridays, Rebecca enjoys ballroom dancing.

Key #3: Create convenience.

Charley is often heard to say, "This week, I really need to get to the gym." Of course, he doesn't always make it. It is the inconvenience of going to and from the gym, and waiting for the equipment to be free, which holds him back.

On the other hand, I use a strategy to fit exercise in every day. I have often typed on my laptop while riding a stationary bicycle at the same time.

Key #4: Minimize the time investment.

Mary finds that she devotes 40 minutes driving to and from the fitness center, 20 minutes changing clothes, and one hour working out. It is no wonder that she procrastinates. As an alternative, you can include short time-period activities in your schedule: a 20-minute walk, a 20-minute session using an exercise video, a 30-minute jog, or 10 minutes using hand-weights. Many people use part of their lunch hour. Another time-saver is to combine a different activity with exercise. You can walk with a friend. When riding a stationary bicycle, you could enjoy watching TV—or listening to an educational audio program.

Key #5: Create your enjoyment.

Have you found that procrastination causes a disruption in your exercise plans? Researchers have observed that when people anticipate discomfort, they often procrastinate in doing a particular task. The important thing to remember is to make exercise an enjoyable part of your daily life. You can enjoy exercise by 1) listening to music during any exercise, 2) walking or jogging with a friend, 3) watching TV while on a stationary bicycle, or 4) reading when using a stationary bicycle or treadmill.

* * * * * *

Sleep Well

Bob Hope, at 80 years old, was still touring and giving shows. Desi Arnaz (of the classic television show I Love Lucy) asked him how he did that. Bob explained that he developed the ability to sleep anywhere. Bob slept on helicopters when he traveled to wherever

American troops were stationed. To perform at his best during his USO shows, Bob was certain to be well-rested. Sleep is a vital part of the exercise process. Your body needs to recover.

Harrison Ford, in preparing for *Indiana Jones and the Last Crusade,* enlisted the coaching of Jake Steinfeld, founder of Body by Jake. Steinfeld helped Ford develop stamina and develop a trim physique. Similarly, every actor who works in action films needs stamina. With precise exercise, we increase our physical capacity. If you're not in the position to engage a personal fitness coach, you can take advantage of videos and books. Consult your doctor before you start a physical fitness regimen.

What the Director is Thinking (about the actor's fatigue level)

If a director sees an actor appearing sleepy, she will worry that the actor may spoil a crucial take. With action scenes, a sleepy actor can also cost a life! Every professional needs to learn how to ensure that she gets the sleep and rest she needs. To maintain your personal safety on the set, you need to be alert and well-rested. Here are methods for going to sleep with more ease.

1. Avoid exercise or television two hours before sleep.

Dr. Deepak Chopra, best-selling author of The Ultimate Happiness Prescription: 7 Keys to Joy and Enlightenment, emphasizes the need to reduce stimulation before sleep. That's the reason to eliminate exercise or television in the two-hour period before your bedtime. It's best to develop a slowing-down ritual for bedtime. For example, dim the lights.

2. Practice relaxation.

Settle back. Start the following relaxation process at your scalp. Tense it for five seconds and then release. In your mind say an affirmation like "My scalp relaxes." Some of my clients say something like "God relaxes my scalp." Use any affirmation that feels comfortable to you. Then go down your body, tensing and then relaxing (your neck, then shoulders, etc. – until you relax your feet). Research demonstrates that after doing a relaxation pattern, people are 25% more relaxed.

3. Enjoy Affirm-Breathing.

After relaxing your muscles, do a pattern that I call *Affirm-Breathing:*

a) Choose an affirmation like "God relaxes me" or "I am peaceful."

b) Breathe in and repeat the affirmation in your mind.

c) Hold your breath for the duration of one affirmation.

d) Breathe out for the duration of two affirmations—and visualize all tension draining from your body, through your bed, and into the ground where it dissipates harmlessly. (Some people imagine that tension is like muddy water draining from their body.)

e) Repeat the process ten times.

4. Begin a Deep Breath-plus-Countdown Process.

Gently breathe. Upon the next breath, think of "10" as you exhale. Breathe in again and think of "9." Continue the process: 8, 7, 6, 5, 4, 3, 2. At "1," just keep repeating "one" in your mind. Some people keep "one" as their mantra while meditating.

5. Focus on "I'll meditate until I fall asleep."

Researchers have noted that those who do transcendental meditation appear to be twelve years younger biologically than their chronological age. Truly, meditation gives you healing rest and recovery. To meditate you can focus on one word like "love" or "peace" or "God." John Gray, best-selling author of *Men Are From Mars, Women Are From Venus,* guides his seminar participants to repeat the phrase "Oh God, my heart is open to you. Please come and sit in my heart" silently as they meditate. Here's the crucial idea: when you tell yourself, "I'll meditate until I fall asleep," you have taken off the pressure of "trying to go to sleep." No longer do you lie there afraid of the sleep that you're missing. You realize that you are experiencing needed rest.

6. Carefully choose your pillow.

Various types of pillows provide support good support and comfort for your head and neck. Some pillows that use buckwheat hulls provide two benefits: a) moldable support for your neck and b) keeping your head and neck cooler than traditional pillows.

7. Use sesame oil for massaging your feet.

Dr. Deepak Chopra recommends massaging the soles of your feet with sesame oil as a soothing way to place yourself in a sleep-ready state.

* * * * * *

Ensure Your Excellent Nutrition

Sylvester Stallone carefully chooses his diet based on the character that he is portraying. When he portrayed the highly intelligent main character in the feature film, *F.I.S.T.*, he ate what he called brain food, which included lots of fish.

Since nutrition provides us with energy and is the building block of our bodies, we need to devote disciplined efforts towards nutrition – just as we are disciplined in exercise.

What the Director is Thinking (about the Actor's food choices)

As a director, I watch for warning signs about actors' behaviors. I need actors who are flexible and alert. I know from personal experience that the food that I eat determines my energy level, alertness and mood. If I share a meal with a potential actor in my films, I will note the person's food choices. As an actor on another director's set, I will carefully choose what I eat at lunch time. I eat lightly because I want to avoid afternoon sleepiness. I eat items that are easily digested (more about that in the below paragraphs).

Here are useful ideas that actors can use based on information from researchers.

1. Stay alert; eat protein.

Researchers point out that protein provides glucose, which is used by the brain as fuel. That's why when individuals only have a salad at lunch time, they discover that they become "fuzzy." That's the reason that actors are advised to eat some protein during breakfast and lunch.

2. Stay Alert; consider avoiding red meat.

Researchers say that digesting red meat takes a lot of the body's resources, and leads many individuals to feel sluggish.

3. Replace Vitamin B complex (related to stress).

Let's face it: filmmaking can be stressful. Researchers note that stress depletes one's body of vital elements. Many nutritionists emphasize that Vitamin B complex is essential to health. With current levels of nutrition in our food supply, researchers often state that supplements are required so that your body functions at peak efficiency.

4. Drink water; stay hydrated.

One of best things that I have seen on sets is when team members bring water to actors in the sun. To feel well, we need water. Soft drinks and other drinks are not absorbed as readily as water. It took some effort but now I do not drink soda, instead I drink water with a splash of either lemon or grape juice to provide some flavor.

5. Slow down aging: take antioxidant vitamins and minerals.

All actors are concerned about their appearance. Some actors want to prolong the years in which they can run and jump as action films require. In our bodies, certain molecules, called free radicals, promote breakdown. Antioxidant vitamins and minerals stop the breakdown process (that is, free radicals taking electrons from other atoms). Therefore, devote the time and effort to learning about antioxidant vitamins and minerals and add them to your diet. For example, according to numerous dietitians, blueberries are a good source of antioxidants.

6. Use anti-carcinogens found in tomatoes and Vitamin C.

Carcinogens are those things in our environment that cause cancer. In light of such hazards, we need to we make ourselves resistant to disease. Add tomatoes and Vitamin C to your diet and increase the power of your immune system.

7. Eat light meals and appropriate snacks.

Many people think that skipping meals is a method for reducing weight. Actually, the body goes into a slowdown mode, that is, it reduces calorie usage. It is better to eat a light meal, than to have an appropriate snack two hours later. Dr. Jack Groppel, author of *The Anti-Diet Book,* mentions that a banana with a bit of peanut butter provides appropriate nutrition and energy He points out that the protein in the peanut butter is helpful for brain function. A number of dietitians emphasize avoiding hydrogenated fats. Eating light and having appropriate snacks helps your metabolism stay at a higher rate of functioning. You'll also stay alert.

Points to Remember:

- **Darkest Secret #11: Nobody cares about you. You're merely a cog in their filmmaking machine. You need to make yourself strong physically, emotionally and spiritually. (You're expected to be tough.)**

- **Your Countermeasure:**

To be tough, you need full access to the resources of your body. You need to take care of your health through excellent amounts of sleep, exercise and relaxation (perhaps meditation or quiet time). Make sure you provide yourself with good nutrition.

CHAPTER 12
DARKEST SECRET #12: YOUR BEING A GOOD ACTOR IS NOT GOOD ENOUGH; YOU MUST BE A GOOD NETWORKER, TOO.

To be a good networker, you need to rehearse what phrases and questions you express that help people feel comfortable in your presence.

Get Your Business Card in the Hands of Directors, Producers and Casting Personnel

1. Establish rapport first before handing your card to someone.

Be careful about pressing a business card on a new acquaintance. Some people find that behavior to be reminiscent of a "slimy used car salesman." The overbearing used car salesman will say, "Hi [with an overbearing handshake], I'm George! Here's my business card!"

Instead, be effective by establishing rapport first when you meet someone at a networking event. Consider asking questions like: "So how do you know our host Mark?" or "What have you found to be helpful during this conference?"

2. Ask, "How can we stay in contact?"

After you have created rapport, ask, "How can we stay in contact?" This is a valuable question because you are uniting under the banner of we. If someone asks, "Why?" You can respond: "I'm in contact with hundreds of people. Perhaps someone in my network could be helpful for you."

3. Ask, "Do you have a card?"

I usually follow my question "How can we stay in contact?" with "Do you have a card?" within a moment or two. By asking about the card, I am taking the person off the hook. Often people respond, "Uh, no, I just ran out." Then I respond, "Oh, I'll make you one," and I pull out a 3x5 card. I continue with, "What's your email address? Do you have email at Google or Yahoo?"

4. Say something like: "Good. Let's trade."

When the person replies, "Yes" to my question about her business card, I say, "Good. Let's trade." My tone of voice is light, pleasant, and certain that she will give me her card. People tend to follow your lead when your tone sounds certain.

Bonus Strategy: Add another title to your actor business card.

Unfortunately, there are some stereotypes about actors and models. Some people think that actors only have gifts of appearance or natural talent. The individuals with prejudices against actors fail to realize that actors must study and develop a number of skills. Sometimes, you can gain an advantage by having another title on your business card. If you choose to produce a short film, video or your demo video, you can add producer to your card. You will need to go with your gut feelings about this option. Some people in the film industry feel that this is a good idea because you become a peer instead of a "begging actor."

* * * * * *

Places to Meet Directors, Producers and Casting Personnel

Here are various locations to meet casting decision-makers:

1. Workshops

I recall meeting producer Stephen Simon (*What Dreams May Come,* starring Robin Williams and *Somewhere In Time,* starring Christopher Reeve and Jane Seymour) at a workshop that he was giving. He is nice and approachable. Similarly, I have conducted workshops and have cast actors I have met at my workshops. Consider for a moment: What workshops would producers and directors attend? Workshops on distribution/financing. Consider going to such workshops.

2. Casting director's office

Being a part-time intern in a casting director's office will get you close to the action.

3. Screenings

At a screening, you can have opportunities to meet

various directors and producers who are attending to support their peer's new production. It is vital for you to be friendly and connected with as many people as possible. You want to be seen, and screenings are a valuable part of your self-promotion activities.

4. Association meetings

You can gain access to producers and directors by attending association meetings. Here are some influential associations: Women In Film; Independent Feature Project; National Asian American Telecommunications Association (NAATA); and Film Arts Foundation. People starting in the film industry find that some of the best first contact come through other people who share something in common. We notice women helping women and Asians helping Asians (for example).

5. The industry person's office

Someone (I'll call "Sandra") took a class in which the instructor set an assignment: choose an industry person you want to meet and do so before the end of the semester. Sandra was working as a temporary assistant at a major studio. In frustration, she complained out loud, "I'll never meet Lynda Obst." Then her employer said, "Lynda Obst? She's on this lot. Her office is nearby." Sandra called Lynda's office and explained her class assignment. She said the right words in the right tone, and was invited to walk over. She met Lynda Obst briefly, and got an "A" in the class. Having a class assignment is a great excuse to meet an important mover and shaker.

6. Film Festivals

Here are some film festivals:

a) Mill Valley Film Festival
b) Sundance Film Festival
c) Telluride Film Festival
d) Berlin Film Festival
e) Cannes Film Festival
f) Milan Film Festival
g) American Film Market

When you start to network at a film festival, keep in mind what the casting decision-makers are focused on. A director or producer is often focused on getting a number of distributors interested in making bids for the distribution rights to her film. Consider getting to know distributors. For example, I met a number of distributors when I attended the American Film Market in Santa Monica, California. By the way, if you introduce an independent filmmaker to a distributor, you may make the filmmaker a friend for life!

You must make hanging out at a film festival pay off for you. That is, remember you're not there to eat, you're there to connect with people. Meeting new people at a film festival can be a daunting task for some people. I can empathize because I began as a shy kid playing the piano for seniors at a retirement home. At nine years old, I was so terrified that I would make a mistake that my leg shook terribly.

In later years, at a networking event, I would push myself to go meet new people. I developed a system: I drew up a 3x5 card with 10 numbered blank lines. After meeting a new person, I would write their name on a blank line. Then I'd tell myself "Nine more to go" and force myself to go meet the next person. I basically made myself talk to people to fill out the slots on that card. Do what is necessary to get yourself to stretch and meet new people.

By the way, here is a technique I share with clients and graduate students: Go to the buffet table, that's where the shy people are. Start up a conversation by asking a simple question that's easy for the other person to answer. You could say something like:

a) Wow. Look at all the desserts. Which one appeals to you?
b) Hello. I'm curious. How did you hear about this event?

* * * * * *

The Excellent Networker follows up and Avoids Being a Pest

1. Use various modes of connecting.
Don't just telephone a casting director once a week. It becomes "old," and the person gets tired of it. Use postcards, email and other methods to keep your name and face in front of casting decision-makers.

2. Find out something that can help the casting personnel.
The owner of an agency that does casting wants new clients. If you go out of your way to discover which companies are filming industrial videos and need them cast, you'll help the agency by alerting them to an opportunity. How do you find out who needs actors for an industrial video? You talk with friends/contacts in various industries. Somewhere in the conversation, you can ask whether their company uses videos for clients or internal training.

Here is an example of how "Joan" brought a lead to a casting agency owner:

Joan (an actress): Hello, Susan, I may have a lead for you.

Susan (a casting agency owner): Oh?

Joan: I discovered that Big Company, Inc. is shooting industrial videos. Are they one of your accounts yet?

Susan: No.

Joan: Well, the person to contact over there is Mary Smith.

Susan: Thank you!

Now Susan will probably place Joan higher on her list of people to call first for acting opportunities.

3. Use a calendar to plan when you will send an email, postcard, or supporting materials.

Do not overdo the number of times you contact an agency in your efforts to secure work. Once a month is good. If you are working to get a specific role, then you can follow your own intuition about possibly using other methods: 1) email, 2) a postcard, or 3) supporting materials. You might visit the office with "a couple of things for my file" that may include: a newspaper article of you performing in a local production or perhaps a color photocopy of the poster of the movie you are in. If you and a friend make a short film, definitely create a poster for it.

* * * * * *

How to Get and Use Testimonials for Your Website and Postcard

Testimonials are useful for an actor's website. In addition, you can send a copy of such a letter to a casting decision-maker after you have established initial contact. Casting decision-makers expect that your first contact will be a headshot with a resume attached. You can use a testimonials page or a testimonial letter as support material. You can also place testimonial quotes on a postcard (one quote is enough for a postcard).

How to Get Testimonials

a) Before you call the person, write up a rough draft of the testimonial you want. Here is an example (of a testimonial that I received): "I strongly recommend Tom Marcoux as an actor for your feature film. I have cast him in multiple projects, and he always comes through for me. Tom has great range as an actor. On the set, I have seen him express tears in one scene and later do a stand-up comedy improvisation."

b) Call the person on the phone. Ask to talk with her for five minutes about a testimonial quote. Say that you want to make your services available to more people like her, and would she please help by providing a few words. Say that you will type up a version of it and send it to her for approval via email.

c) When she approves, type up the letter. Go to her office and photocopy the letter onto her stationery. With this process, you are making it easy for her to merely "okay" the letter (which is how to ask for someone to sign the letter). The word "sign" is ominous – like "sign your life away." People are happy to "okay" things. Notice how you're making it easy for her to say "yes", and you do the work, so you're not kept waiting.

d) Do not ask her to write and type the letter. Many people are reluctant to write and are slow to write something. Take the writing out of their hands and make the whole process quick and easy for them.

Vital Details for an Effective Testimonial

a) Have the testimonial tell a story. Remember: stories sell, facts just tell. How can a testimonial sound like a story? Here's an example: "On the set of One Rough Night, Jean Mithay was so creative. She ad-libbed a line that improved the scene."

b) Focus on specifics. If you have worked with the person five times, include that.

Points to Remember:

- **Darkest Secret #12: Your being a good actor is NOT good enough; you must be a good networker, too.**

- **Your Countermeasure:**

Learn how to effectively get your business card into the hands of directors, producers and other casting personnel. In addition, learn to meet people at industry event. Use multiple ways to stay in touch with your new contacts.

•

CHAPTER 13
DARKEST SECRET #13: NOBODY CARES—SO YOU BETTER BE A MASTER AT FOLLOW-UP.

Kate Winslet really wanted the lead role of Rose in *Titanic,* and she did not hesitate in letting Director James Cameron know it. She lobbied the director and called from England. She said, "You don't understand. I am Rose. I don't know why you're even seeing anyone!" James Cameron said, "Kate was so positive and aggressive. It cracked me up. I thought, 'Okay, that's the sort of spirit it's going to take to get through this.'"

To demonstrate your burning desire for a role, you can use a day planner, or perhaps Google Calendar, to plan your follow-up.

When you want a part, make sure that you get the director to know it. It is now legendary that Elijah Wood dressed up as a Hobbit to encourage director Peter Jackson to cast him as Frodo in *The Lord of the Rings*. Elijah wore breeches and a flowing shirt and went out into the hills to shoot his audition video.

Audrey Meadows, who portrayed Alice in *The Honeymooners* television show, secured the role through excellent follow-up. After she met Jackie Gleason (the show's star and producer), she asked Jackie's colleague about Jackie's reaction to her. Jackie felt that Audrey was "all wrong—she's too young and too pretty! I'll give you she's charming, witty, neat and smart—everything that Alice Kramden is not."

Audrey wanted this role so she called for a photographer to take photos of her the very next morning. Audrey told the photographer that he'd "have to develop and print them by the afternoon so we can get them up to Jackie the same day. They're going to have to make their minds up pretty quickly because they only have a little over two weeks before he goes on air, so we have to work fast."

The next morning, the photographer arrived and took photos of Audrey with no makeup, hair a mess, and a tattered blouse. That afternoon, Jackie's colleague presented the photos without identifying the actress. Jackie exclaimed, "That's our Alice! Who is she? Where is she? Can we get her?" His colleague replied, "That's the girl who was here yesterday, Audrey Meadows, and she arranged the photo shoot to show she could look the part as well as play it."

"Hire her," Jackie said. What we learn from Audrey's successful effort is that we need to follow-up quickly in a timely manner—and we need to follow our own hunches.

What the Director is Thinking (about Follow-up for Success)

When an actor calls my office more than once, I often think, "Oh, this actor really does want the part." Any director feels that an actor with a blasé attitude toward a part will put in a blasé performance. So stay in touch! Do it subtly with a postcard or an occasional email.

It's important to note that you can score points with a director or producer by expressing your commitment and enthusiasm for a role. The director or producer may need a new injection of enthusiasm by that point. For example, James L. Brooks took two years to raise the money for *Terms of Endearment*. "Everyone turned it down twice," said actress Shirley MacLaine. Shirley continued by adding her comments about acting:

"The spirit of the moment is everything—not the intellect. It's the combination of the moment, mind, body and spirit." She noted, "A good actor certainly listens....Acting is always reacting....Bette Davis said, 'Start the character parts early so you have a long career.'"

Three Methods to Follow up with the Casting Decision-Maker

1. Use email effectively.

As I have mentioned earlier, find some way to be helpful to the casting decision-maker. If you find an article that might help her in some way, you can send an email with a link to it.

2. Send a thank you postcard

Send a thank you postcard immediately after an audition. Do not send a letter. No one has the time to read something long. Be sure the postcard has your photo on it. Hand-write your brief note. Also include a positive comment such as "I really like the part of Mindy because of her strength. I am excited about the possibility of bringing her to life." Let the director know that you want the part!

3. Remember to use 5 Creative "Touches"

Researchers note that top sales professionals ask for the sale five times. A successful actor plans to use five creative ways to be in touch with the decision-maker including:

1) Meet at a networking event.

2) Send a follow-up note.

3) Audition.

4) Send a thank you postcard.

5) Send an email with useful information.

6) Phone call (You can say something like: "Did you receive my email? Great. Oh, I'm still excited about the role of Joe. What can I do to help this process along?")

7) Send an article mentioning the person (with a note, "Saw this article. Thought you might want a copy for your files").

Do not be a pest. Do be helpful.

Points to Remember:

• **Darkest Secret #13: Nobody cares—so you better be a master at follow up.**

• **Your Countermeasure:**

Develop your own plan for following up with casting decision-makers. Consider email, phone calls, a postcard—and attending events.

CHAPTER 14
DARKEST SECRET #14: EVERYBODY IS TIRED ON SET AND TEMPERS FLARE SO YOU BETTER BE PROFESSIONAL ON THE SET!

How to Talk with an Assistant Director or Director

During one of my seminars, an actor asked, "How do you ask an Assistant Director a question?" It's not as simple as you may think. I will share with you five elements of effectively asking such a question.

First, I'll put this into context. A few months ago, I had a dream that reveals both an actor's dream and an actor's nightmare.

My dream:

I am playing an officer on the bridge of a Star Trek *motion picture. Standing next to me is George Takei ("Mr. Sulu – now Captain Sulu" of the Classic Series). I have the last line of the film, but I don't know what it is! I ask George, and he tells me one version of the line. Trying to help, Gates McFadden ("Dr. Crusher" of* Star Trek: The Next Generation*) offers another* *version. Avery Brooks ("Captain Sisko" of* Star Trek: Deep Space Nine*) mentions a different version of the line! Desperate, I look at the director, but he is an intense young man who is snapping at people because he is under pressure since the production is behind schedule. "Uh-oh," I think, "better not interrupt him now." He looks at the video-assist monitor and watches some footage that has already been shot. I see myself on the screen doing a devastating kick to a stuntman.*

The dream ends…

We can use this dream as a springboard to some important ideas for you to use.

Tip #1: Develop rapport with the Assistant Director before you need him or her.

In the dream, my colleagues, the actors, tried to help me with the line of dialogue, but their information was inaccurate. It would have been good for me to locate the Assistant Director and ask him or her about the line. If the Assistant Director doesn't have the final script in hand, he or she can direct me to the script supervisor.

Tip #2: Stay physically fit.

In the dream, I saw the director was screening some previous footage on a video assist monitor. In the scene that the director viewed, I was doing a fight scene.

In another section of this book, I discuss the actor's resume. It is helpful to include your physical abilities in your "Special Skills" and "Training" portions of your resume. Physical abilities help an actor be more employable. For example, a child-actor I know studied martial arts which led to her role on a show *Kangarate*—about karate.

Tip #3: Go to where the jobs are

If you're currently located in a city outside of Southern California, build up your resume before you consider moving.

Certain productions require that you move to Los Angeles. For example, various television shows are filmed in L.A. If you want to be in a film of the *Star Trek* franchise, you will need to audition for casting directors in Los Angeles, the location of Paramount Studios. With a substantial resume, excellent demo video and related experience, you will be ready for encounters with Los Angeles casting directors.

Now we'll continue with how to ask a question of an Assistant Director.

Here are techniques that I have used as an actor on various sets.

1. Practice your question in your mind before you approach the Assistant Director.

Repeat your question silently a few times. Here are examples: "Hello, I'm Tom and you are...?" and "Would you prefer me to put the bicycle here – or over there?" You notice that in the second question, I provide a "this or that" question. It's easier for someone in a leadership position to answer "Do the second thing" than have to observe the whole situation and come up with an idea on their own.

2. Stand patiently in her sight-line.

Do not interrupt the Assistant Director when she is on her walkie-talkie. Just stand patiently near her where she can see you. When she is ready, she'll turn to you. She will appreciate your good manners as you stand patiently.

3. Offer your name first.

A confident person always offers her name first.

Demonstrate that you are "quietly confident," and offer your name as you approach the Assistant Director. Say "Hi, I'm ___ and you are…?"

4. Be brief.

The Assistant Director is one of the busiest people on the set. Make a friend: be brief.

5. Quickly, gracefully close the discussion.

Smile and say, "Thanks. That's what I needed to know." Then turn and return to your position.

* * * * * *

Worksheet for "How to Talk with an Assistant Director (or Casting Decision-Maker)"

(You can write your answers on a sheet of paper and keep it in your pocket.)

1. Practice your question in your mind before you approach the person.
2. Stand patiently in her sight-line.
3. Offer your name first.
(example: "Hi, I'm Joey Avegard and you are…")
4. Be brief.
(write your question in a brief way)
5. Quickly, gracefully close the discussion.
(example: "That's what I need to know. Thanks." (Turn and return to your waiting place.)

Points to Remember:

- **Darkest Secret #14: Everybody is tired on set and**

tempers flare, so you better be professional on the set!

- **Your Countermeasure:**

To act like a professional on the set, rehearse how you'll ask a question of the Assistant Director or Director. You need to be brief. Consider if using a "this or that" question will help in the particular situation. For example, one could ask a question like: "Would you like me to put this bicycle against the wall or against the lamp post?"

CHAPTER 15
DARKEST SECRET #15: IT'S EASIER TO REJECT YOU THAN TO TAKE THE RISK OF HIRING YOU (SO MASTER TECHNIQUES SO YOU PUT THE OTHER PERSON AT EASE).

Imagine Robert DeNiro is noted for his almost obsessive preparation: for example, learning to play the saxophone for *New York, New York,* directed by Martin Scorsese. The successful actor prepares for auditions.

In the audition, it's your job to convince the casting decision-makers that you are the one actor for the role. For example, Glenn Close was convinced that she was ideal for the role of "Alex" in *Fatal Attraction,* but the producers and director did not even want to meet with her. Fortunately, her agent kept calling. Finally, they had a meeting and Glenn firmly asked to read with the star of the film Michael Douglas. Glenn later said, "I've never had an ego about auditioning. Because I think, especially in movies, the image you can create with one character stays in people's minds. And they have to be convinced that you can do something else."

Finally, when Glenn performed an audition with Michael Douglas the director, Adrian Lyne, and producers Sherry Lansing and Stanley Jaffe were convinced that she had all the elements: the intensity, sexiness and vulnerability.

The successful actor is nearly obsessive about preparation for auditions. She makes sure that she's ready to:

1) Give a cold reading
2) Give "more"
3) Give "less"
4) Find the "beat changes"
5) Tell a bit about yourself (while you're being recorded on video)
6) Improvise

Furthermore, you must take care of yourself and avoid coming across as a "needy actor."

What the Director is Thinking (about Avoid coming across as needy)

You must take care of yourself outside the audition room so that you are at your peak of awareness and flexibility in the audition room. The idea is to come to the audition with a lot of energy. You need to be alert for opportunities to make a good connection with the casting decision-maker. You might even have the opportunity to praise the screenplay. Directors respond to sincere praise. Saying "I like this line" creates a positive energy. You come across as confident and giving when you focus on priorities of the casting personnel in the room. Your confidence shows when you truly act by listening intently and being in the moment.

On the other hand, when we feel needy, we often "broadcast" a certain energy that has people around us feeling uncomfortable, too. Here are methods so that you nurture yourself and release any painful feelings before an audition.

Three Methods to Avoid Coming Across as Needy

1. Release the marbles.

Roger Mellot, author of the best-selling audio program *Stress Management for Professionals,* talks about "releasing marbles." Think of a marble as something that causes you some distress – perhaps a co-worker makes a hurtful, disparaging remark. Through the day, many of us "swallow these marbles." It's no wonder that by the end of the day or week that we feel weighed down or "heavy." When we have hit our limit we may also get sick and spew forth these metaphorical marbles. In an audition situation, spewing marbles may take the form of saying inappropriate things.

Examples of inappropriate marble dumping:

a) "Oh, God, what a day I'm having. You wouldn't believe the rude people that...."

b) "Oh, a birthday. You know my last birthday, my best friend forgot, and I just couldn't..."

To appropriately release our marbles we can:

1) Write in a journal.

2) Talk with a friend.

3) Talk with a counselor.

4) See a sad movie and release some pain through crying.

5) Participate in spiritual activities: prayer, a service or meditation.

6) Experience daily breathing and meditation sessions.

7) Exercise.

8) Sleep an appropriate amount.

Use your day planner to schedule some ways you intend to release marbles appropriately.

2. Select your stories.

When you first meet someone, your stories will convey whether you're needy or not. Some of us have become habitual poor me storytellers. Author Roger Mellot used to tell a story of how his brother died when he was a young boy. One woman asked, "Why did you tell me that story?" Later, Roger realized that he was looking for sympathy. He doesn't tell that story as much.

An effective person greeting someone for the first time tells stories of how she is enjoying her life. She tells stories filled with fun and hope.

Now it's your turn. In your personal journal, identify one of your stories that you need to drop from your discussions with people you're meeting for the first time.

3. Uplift your language.

Some phrases that we say habitually drag down a conversation. Let go of phrases such as:

a) "You know what happened to me: I was stuck in traffic for an hour!"

b) "That sales clerk ignored me!"

Replace them with empowering phrases like:

a) "Here's some good news...."

b) "Something good that happened today was...."

c) "I'm looking forward to____ because it's fun to ____"

Identify a 'down-energy' phrase that you want to let go. Note in your personal journal a replacement phrase that uplifts your feelings. When you feel better, you naturally uplift the energy in a conversation.

4. Develop a support system.

Have you ever met someone who gushes personal information too soon? Did they complain about a lot of things? This person really needs a support system. If, at the moment, you're in a new area and are just developing new friendships, then you can consider engaging a counselor or therapist, if appropriate.

A special note about counselors: an effective counselor can help you see your actions with a different perspective and help you discover new actions for personal growth. Be wary of counselors whose approach only dwells on your past pain. Instead, you can feel empowered when you learn from your pain, stop ineffective patterns, and move on.

People are a vital part of our support system, but for various reasons, they are often unavailable. So it's important that you include Solo-Actions as part of your support system. Solo-actions are activities that you can do on your own. Think of when a new pilot goes for a solo flight. A new pilot may feel fear at the beginning of a solo-flight, but later she can feel exhilarated. I encapsulate this idea with this phrase: "Flying Solo is not being lonely."

Here are some Solo-actions:

- Enjoy a hobby. You can do hobbies when you want and when you need to. A hobby fulfills a deep need for self-expression.
- Read a book. Novels are fun. You can read nonfiction to expand your knowledge.
- Exercise. You can take a walk when you want to—and you'll feel better, today, and tomorrow!
- Listen to an energizing audio program.
- Take yourself out. You can go to museums, a movie, a

workshop solo! (Solo is a powerful word that's much better than all by myself).

With a hobby, a book, or an audio program, you're feeding your spirit. Doing your hobby (like painting) for merely 15 minutes a day can color your whole day bright and happy!

Train yourself. Invest in yourself. Buy educational audio programs; go to night classes. Get a coach. The more you know, the more you can do, and the more self-esteem you feel.

What Solo-actions will help you feel nurtured? Write down your answers in your day planner, and schedule some for this week.

What's the opposite of "needy"? It's when you radiate charisma.

A number of people think that charisma is the characteristic of someone who "seizes people's attention." That can be one form.

Here we'll talk about two types of charisma:

a) "Seizing people's attention"

b) "Setting people at ease and getting them to feel good!"

In Hollywood, people work again and again with people that they're comfortable with. So the "setting people at ease and feeling good" form of charisma can translate directly into you getting more work.

Here are three methods related to that form of charisma as "setting people at ease and getting them to feel good":

1. Strive to be interested.

So many actors try to be "interesting," and they come off as self-absorbed braggarts. Instead, be sure to "be in the moment," listening with full attention. Demonstrate you're interested. Then you'll put the other person at ease and they can enjoy expressing themselves in your presence.

2. Ask good, gentle questions.

How do you get the other person to talk about himself or the project? You ask gentle questions. A gentle question demonstrates that you're paying attention to someone's feelings and you're gently asking to hear more. It is the opposite of hard questioning that sounds like an interrogation.

Here are examples of gentle questions:

- That sounds like it was frustrating. So what did you do next?
- So what brought you to this screenplay? What about it captured your attention?
- In order for you to know someone is ideal for this part, what has to happen?

3. Make the person feel like the most important person in the room

I attended a private luncheon where President Bill Clinton gave a speech. I had not been impressed with televised video of Bill Clinton because he came across as "too slick." But in person, he was truly charismatic. He gave full attention to every person he talked with. He made the person feel like he or she was the most important person in the room.

Pretend that every single person you meet has a sign around his or her neck that says, "Make me feel important." Not only will you succeed in sales, you will succeed in life. — Mary Kay Ash

So an important part of being charismatic is to radiate your interest, approval and appreciation of the person you're talking with. This is something you can practice. You can lean a bit forward and nod. Let the person know that you're listening by saying things like "uh-huh." You can ask gentle questions. Start practicing with friend today.

* * * * * *

Two Methods to Easily Recover from a Conversation Mistake

During a series of auditions I ran for one of my feature films, one actress came in and made an embarrassing error. I asked the actor to move a chair to the hallway. The person did so and then sat in the chair – in the hallway. I heard someone chuckle in the room. This actress merely said, "Oh, now I understand" and returned to the room. The actor stayed in the moment, and then gave a great performance. I appreciated how this actress was flexible, and quickly recovered from making a "mistake." She got the part!

Mistakes happen. Chris Pine (who played Captain Kirk in the J.J. Abrams' feature film *Star Trek*) said that he auditioned for the lead role of Jake Sully of James Cameron's *Avatar*. Chris Pine said, "It was my worst audition ever." Okay. But Chris Pine bounced back and has appeared as a lead actor in a number of feature films since then.

What the Director is Thinking (about Recovering from a mistake)

The director is looking for adaptable actors. As a director, I'm looking for that magic—that extra something that the actor brings to the film. I have a vision for the film, and I want my vision or better. I prefer to see an actor take a risk, because I know there is always take two. Often, on my set, I'll tell an actor, "We're covered. We have that last take in the can. Now, in this take, go wild. Try something different."

In an audition, I'm hoping to find a flexible actor. A flexible actor can make an incredible contribution to a film. For example, for *Willy Wonka and the Chocolate Factory*, Gene Wilder insisted that he, as Willy Wonka, do a "crippled walk" trick. The scene is the entrance of Willy Wonka to the film. Wonka steps out of the factory door and painfully limps toward the crowd of onlookers waiting to see the reclusive, mystery man. Seeing Wonka's apparent injury or deformity, the crowd goes quiet.

Suddenly, Wonka tilts forward sure to fall on his face, but he does an agile forward roll instead. The crowd gasps in astonishment. And so did the movie theater audience when I saw the film the first time. Gene's crippled walk trick was a tremendous contribution; Gene said that he wanted the character introduced as someone whose actions were completely unpredictable.

To be natural and charismatic during an audition, you need a good level of comfort. Then you'll be able to flow with the situation and take appropriate risks. To ensure your comfort, prepare yourself to recover from any possible conversation mistake. Here are two methods:

Method #1: Use the phrase: "That's not what I meant to say. What I meant is..."

If you say something that comes out in a way that you don't like, you can immediately say: "That's not what I meant to say. What I meant is..." And you rephrase what you just said. Be sure to practice this *Recovery Phrase*. By the way, it is one of the first things I teach my clients and graduate students during my public speaking class. I invite you to say it out loud now. Only by practicing the recovery phrase does it become natural and one of your tools.

Method #2: Use the phrase "Forgive me, I was just...."

Marshall Sylver, author of *Passion, Profit and Power,* points out that you can recover from a conversational error by saying, "Forgive me, I was just..." His usual example is about the overeager salesperson who tries to close a sale too soon. The salesperson can say, "Forgive me, I was just so excited about how you'll enjoy feeling the power of this car..." Marshall points out that saying "forgive me" creates a connection with someone you have just met. Why? Because you are asking for participation. People tend to reply: "sure" or "okay."

* * * * * *

Three Methods to Be Seen as an Interesting Person

Actors hope that casting decision-makers find them interesting and generalize that feeling to an impression that audiences will find them fascinating, too.

One way to make that good first impression is to prepare your stories about some interesting experiences that you had. For example, actor Dennis Farina was a police officer. Numerous casting directors know this detail. And Farina portrayed the lead villain in *Midnight Run,* starring Robert DeNiro and Charles Grodin. One of Farina's first successful roles was as a police officer in the TV anthology series *Police Story.* We can imagine that Dennis always mentioned his first career as a police officer in an audition. He continued to successfully play characters that were either police officers or criminals.

What the Director is Thinking (about an Actor as an interesting person)

Many directors want actors who have done some living. An actor who has endured a divorce may bring extra textures to the role of a person going through a divorce. Before you attend an audition, make a plan about what you will talk about. Think of how you can relate your personal history to some aspect of the character for which you're auditioning. If part of your personal biography relates to the character's background, share that detail.

1. Listen first.

Dale Carnegie, the author of the classic *How to Win Friends and Influence People,* shared this secret: be sincerely interested in the other person, and he or she will find you fascinating.

2. Write up your 25-second commercial.

Brian Tracy, author and self-made millionaire, notes that people tend to think at the rate of 500 words per minute—while the average person talks at 100 words per minute. So while you're talking, the other person can be easily distracted by her own thoughts. Brian advises that we express ideas for a couple of seconds and then ask a question to keep our listener tuned in. Here's an example of how to use a "25-second commercial" during a networking event.

Sandy: "That's a nice pin."

Amanda: "Thanks. It reminds me of acting on the set of *Winter Songs,* the feature film. So are you looking for something particular—for this role?"

Amanda: "You were in *Winter Songs*?"

Now, Amanda has slipped in an interesting detail, and

she has avoided giving a personal monologue. During an audition, use your 25-second commercial in response to the director's request: "So tell me about yourself." Write out your response and rehearse it. I have been amazed when I have seen other actors stammer their way through their response as it is recorded on video. The actor can lose opportunities due to this lack of preparation:

a) The stammering may convince the director that person will be terrible in TV interviews when movie promotion activities begin.

b) The stammering may convince a casting director that the actor is unable to be an effective spokesperson for any product.

In your personal journal, note two of your best credits, one interesting life experience, and two special skills. Now, use these elements to form your personal 25-second commercial.

3. Turn your body toward the person.

People feel that you are interested in them when you look like you're interested. Turn your body so that you're facing the person, and she will feel like she has your attention.

In my public speaking classes, I emphasize this idea: "heart faces heart."

Points to Remember:

• Darkest Secret #15: It's easier to reject you than to take the risk of hiring you (so master techniques so you put the other person at ease).

• **Your Countermeasure:**

Avoid coming across as needy. Learn to make the other person feel important. Rehearse your "25-second commercial about yourself" so that you come across as confident and professional.

CHAPTER 16
DARKEST SECRET #16: REJECTION IS A HUGE PART OF AN ACTOR'S LIFE. YOU BETTER BECOME SKILLED IN DEALING WITH IT.

One "If you don't take risks, you don't gain anything," Bridget Fonda emphasized to an auditorium of young actors. She said that she was "awkward and uncomfortable" when she first acted in high school. When she studied acting at the Lee Strasberg Theatre Institute, she felt doubtful about her decision to make a career of acting. "What I had was beyond stage fright. I'd go onstage, and later I couldn't remember a thing. I'd think, I'm the worst person in this class," she recalled. Even when a tough acting teacher humiliated her, Bridget persisted. "When you find something you care about, you have to take chances, even making yourself into a fool. And one day, I decided I'd do whatever I wanted. That was it! Suddenly the teacher was saying, 'Yes!' and I was no longer scared." Bridget Fonda has been in over 30 motion pictures since 1987. The amount of her work is only matched by her renowned grandfather,

Henry Fonda, over a similar period.

Michael Caine is a well-respected actor and the winner of the Oscar for his role in *Cider House Rules*. However, many critics have complained that Michael has been in a number of "poor films." (*Jaws IV*, anyone?) Michael's response is: "I chose the best project available at the time." He loves to work. Through the many performances, he has honed his craft.

Four Methods to Bounce Back from Rejection

Jessica Lange first burst on the acting scene as "Dwan" in the remake of *King Kong* in the 1970's. Then she couldn't find work for two years. No one took her seriously; they thought that she was as dim as the character Dwan. Then, in one year she had the lead role of *Frances*, and her (Oscar-winning) role in *Tootsie* (starring Dustin Hoffman). Her ex-lover and director Bob Fosse said, "I have never seen someone go from cold to really hot so fast." She had to keep on auditioning to have a chance at these career-making roles.

We never know what it is that will put a particular actor over the top. Charlton Heston won the part of Moses in *The Ten Commandments* by a nose. His broken nose was injured in college football. With his intense research, Director Cecil B. De Mille noticed that Michelangelo's statue of Moses has his nose broken in the same place as Charlton Heston's nose. So casting can be that arbitrary.

With casting so hit-and-miss, how can you keep up your own morale? Hold on to these ideas: You always win when you put in a good effort. Winning is in the effort—results are often out of our hands. You might say they're in the hands of Higher Power. You're a "winning actor" when you demonstrate in the audition that you are helpful and cooperative. For example, Orson Welles was directing Charlton Heston in a night scene of *Touch of Evil*. The sun was rising fast. Orson called out from the other side of a bridge, "Quick, Chuck, run across the bridge!"

"Orson, I will," said Charlton, "—but can you tell me why?"

"Just do it," Orson pleaded, "—and I'll tell you why when you get here."

Charlton ran across the bridge.

Make sure to cultivate a reputation as a cooperative actor. Let's face it. There are times when the director wants the actor to "just do it."

What the Director is Thinking (on Actors bouncing back after rejection)

A director is looking for an actor who really wants the part. As a director, I'm looking for someone who will go the extra mile. Filmmaking is vigorous—especially when I'm filming action scenes. When given sides (your character's dialogue given before an audition), demonstrate that you want the part by memorizing the lines. Barbara Hershey (*The Right Stuff, Hannah and Her Sisters,* and *The Natural*) said, "If [you really want] a part, don't read—memorize. Don't come in with your face in a piece of paper, come in as close as you can to what you think the character might be. . . . I think acting is telling the truth and as much truth as you can assemble. If they're not going to give it to you, give it to yourself. Go in as much as you can with your concept of the character. If you don't have a clear concept of the character, choose one so that you can be specific. Often directors in readings don't direct, they'll say, 'Thank you very much' as if that's it. Sometimes I think they don't have a clear concept of what they want, and yet they want to get their socks knocked off."

So let's use Barbara Hershey's advice as inspiration. When you memorize your lines, you'll feel good about your efforts. And this relates to the first of the following three methods so you bounce back from rejection and learn something along the way.

1. Use a *Did Well/Area to Improve Journal*.

To keep up my own morale, I keep a *Did Well/Area to Improve Journal*. After every audition in which I participate as an actor, I write down what I did well. Then I note an area to improve. I always succeed in an audition—because I'm always learning something, and I'm rehearsing for the next crucial audition. That's how I use my Did Well/Area to Improve Journal.

2. Flow through the mourning process.

The mourning process has been shown to have stages. Feeling rejected when you don't get a part can trigger our grieving. Elisabeth Kübler-Ross described what she called the Five Stages of Grief:

a) Denial
b) Anger
c) Bargaining
d) Depression
e) Acceptance

Often, we need to flow through the mourning process and through the five stages so we can bounce back from disappointments. Many processes can be helpful, like journal writing, seeing a counselor, joining a support group, or talking with a trusted friend. Sometimes, it comes down to giving yourself a chance to cry. I have found sad movies to be helpful for this.

Each individual is different. Here's an example. Sandra does not get the lead role in a feature film. She wrote the following thoughts in her journal:

a) "What? No. They just didn't get to see the side of me that could play this role!" [Denial]

b) "Well, damn them if they can't see what a good actress I am!" [Anger]

c) "Maybe if I call them nicely, then they'll give me another audition." [Bargaining]

d) "Oh, hell. They saw it. I'm no good. I'm not talented enough." [Depression]

e) "We didn't have a match. So I don't match the idea they had in mind. I'm persistent. There are other roles out there for me." [Acceptance]

There's plenty of rejection going around. You need to keep up your own energy so it helps to become good at flowing through your own grieving process.

3. Reward yourself for the effort.

One of my acting mentors said, "You've done the job for the day, when you've completed the audition." This reminds me that the effort of attending the audition is valuable and noteworthy. We keep up our own morale by rewarding ourselves for the effort. Results are often out of our hands. But we can control how many contacts we make and how many auditions we apply for.

Your inner child (emotional self) is the source of your energy. Keep your inner child happy by rewarding yourself for making the effort to prepare and participate in an audition. Also praise yourself in your Did Well/Area to

Improve Journal.

4. Create a "Celebrate Someone Disagrees" Ritual.

Every actor gets rejected for some part that she knows she's ideal for. What do you do when you're feeling down? You can grieve for a time. And then it's helpful to have a way to reframe the situation. To "reframe" means to shift your interpretation.

So when an actor gets "rejected" for a role, it is not the actor-as-a-person who is rejected. In fact, you can take it to another level and tell yourself "someone disagrees that I'm right for the role." When I have received a negative review for one of my projects, I tell myself: "Someone disagrees about whether the article [for example] is useful to him." Then I do a "Celebrate Someone Disagrees" Ritual. That is, I reward myself for having the courage to raise "my voice" in the world.

You can include someone with your "CSD-Ritual" or you can do something kind for yourself. For example, my sweetheart often listens to my writing. So if I get a negative review, we often go to See's Candies because chocolate means "celebration" to her.

The truth is: successful people expect to be "rejected" sometimes. They don't let that slow them down. And you can encourage yourself to go out for more auditions. How? Plan to reward yourself for every rejection. Pre-plan your "Celebrate Someone Disagrees" Ritual.

Points to Remember:

- **Darkest Secret #16: Rejection is a huge part of an actor's life. You better become skilled in dealing with it.**

• **Your Countermeasure:**

Use your Did Well/Area to Improve journal to learn from each audition and to prepare for the next one. Flow through the mourning process, and reward yourself for your courage and efforts.

CHAPTER 17
DARKEST SECRET #17: PEOPLE HIRE THE ONES THEY'RE COMFORTABLE WITH. EVEN IF YOU'RE THE MOST QUALIFIED, THAT DOES NOT INSURE YOU WILL GET THE PART.

First, you need to develop your craft of acting. Secondly, and just as important, you need to learn to put people at ease in your presence. Then they'll like you and feel good when near you. That leads to more acting opportunities.

Your Countermeasure: Put them at ease.

Six ways to Put the Person at Ease with You Based on Personality Styles

When George Takei (Mr. Sulu of *Star Trek*) first met Gene Roddenberry (creator of *Star Trek*) in an informal meeting, Gene was late.

"I hope it wasn't too long," Gene said. "Oh no, not at all," George said politely.

"How do you pronounce that last name of yours?" Gene asked as he mispronounced the

name.

George replied that it rhymes with okay.

"Oh, okay. Takei as in okay. Takei is okay," Gene laughed.

George flowed in the moment and mentioned that the way Gene pronounced his name is a "legitimate Japanese word."

"Oh, really? What does it mean?" Gene asked.

"Well, it translates into English as 'expensive.'"

"Oh my God! I'd better make sure I call you Takei. Takei is definitely okay," Gene said, laughing.

George demonstrated methods for helping the other person become comfortable.

As a side note: Years later, George Takei suggested that I cut a scene from a feature film I was set to direct. I showed him storyboards in which a tear fell from a character's face into a tea cup. George gently said, "Uh, Tom. Isn't that a bit melodramatic." Thank you, George. I never filmed it.

1. Do not complain.

Years later, George explained that he lied when he said that he had not waited long to Gene Roddenberry. George avoided putting Gene on the defensive.

2. Create a comfortable dialogue and use humor if appropriate.

George flowed in the moment, following Gene's lead. George noted Gene's personality style of spontaneity and warmth. So George spoke of "expensive" and created an opportunity for them to share laughter.

What the Director is Thinking (about Personality Styles)

A director is looking for someone who is easy to be around. People tend to like others who seem similar in temperament. So if you're around a pragmatic, blunt person, then be concise in your comments. If you're around a director who has an analytic style, provide the details she craves.

Read the person's Personality Style.

A number of researchers and authors have noted what appear to be consistent personality types: 1) The Director, 2) The Analyzer, 3) The Relater, and 4) The Socializer. For years, I have been teaching audiences these details and I have found that combining the labels with animal names is useful as a mnemonic device. This section is a combination of my own research and the observations of other authors including Tony Alessandra, Michael J. O'Connor and Roger Dawson.

We discover a new person's personality style by listening very closely to what a person says. They provide you with clues. It is important to note the person's style so that you can understand, create rapport and set the person at ease. Now, let's explore the characteristics that form the four personality styles. Workshop participants sometimes notice that people can be a combination of these traits, with usually one dominant style.

3. Provide a "Director" with a concise, bottom-line summary.

We make a "Director" (also whom I call "Lion") feel comfortable by providing a concise, bottom-line summary when we tell a story or make a point.

How to tell if someone is a Director (Lion):

1) Does the person speak bluntly and quickly and does she finish people's sentences?

2) Does the person show impatience when she perceives weakness in someone?

3) Does the person mostly emphasize results and the bottom line?

What excites them? Action

Greatest Failing: Can't Stand Weakness

Greatest Fear: Failing to get progress and/or being soft on others

Tip on unspoken expectations: Wants you to interact with her in a quick, to-the-point way.

4. Listen to the Analyzer's details; be precise in your descriptions.

We make an Analyzer ("Beaver") comfortable by 1) letting them tell us the in-depth details, and 2) not pressuring them to give the short summary. When we are also precise and provide details in our description, the Analyzer will feel that we are similar to him or her.

How to tell if someone is an Analyzer:

1) Is the person slow in making decisions while demanding all the details?

2) Does the person seem too critical about details?

3) Does the person go overboard with expressing details?

What excites them? Reason

Greatest Failing: Too Critical

Greatest Fear: Being perceived as stupid or making mistakes

Tip on unspoken expectations: Wants to see the in-depth facts

5. Show the Relater you have similar interests.

The Relater ("Dog") enjoys talking with someone with similar interests. The Relater is also allergic to pressure, so when you ask questions do it gently.

How to tell if someone is a Relater:

1) Does the person attempt to duck pressure?

2) Does the person demonstrate a lot of concern over people being happy or not?

3) Is the person a slow decision-maker?

4) Does the person accept too much work and have trouble saying "no"?

What excites them? Feeling comfortable and connected to people

Greatest Failing: Slow decision-maker, avoids pressure, unable to say "no" and has too much work

Greatest Fear: People being unhappy

Tips on unspoken expectations:

1) Interested in the people factor—how a proposal will be accepted by the team and how individuals will be affected.

2) Wants you to be friendly—to take a few moments to chat: person to person

6. Make the Socializer feel comfortable by showing how you like him or her.

We make the Socializer ("Peacock") feel comfortable by showing how we like him or her. Consider phrases like:

a) "I like how you did…"

b) "That sounds like you did a great job…"

Only talk about what you sincerely appreciate.

How to tell if someone is a Socializer:

1) Does the person have poor follow-up?

2) Does the person seem that he is concerned that people like him?

3) Is the person a fast decision-maker who wants to feel good?

What excites them? Tossing around ideas

Greatest Failing: Being "flaky" and inconsistent

Greatest Fear: Not being liked or left out of the "action"

Tips on unspoken expectations:

1) may often expect you to handle the details

2) would like to know (in little ways) that you like him

3) would expect you to listen to her if she's tossing around ideas

4) would like it if you helped with follow-up

* * * * * *

Worksheet for Preparing to talk with the 4 Personality Styles:

Step 1. If the person is a Director ("Lion"):

1) How can you interact with her in a quick, to-the-point way (with a written agenda)?

2) How can you show her that you are strong, too? (that is, you are unruffled by circumstances)

3) How can you emphasize results and the bottom line?

Step 2. If the person is a Analyzer ("Beaver"):

1) How can you show that you're producing high-quality work?

2) How can you show that you approach things from the rational side?

3) How can you present in-depth facts?

Step 3. If the person is a Relater ("Dog"):

1) How can you show that you have similar interests?

2) How can you, in your words and actions, show that you're not a source of pressure?

Step 4. If the person is an Socializer ("Peacock"):

1) How can you help with the details?

2) How can you (in little ways) show that you like him/her?

3) How can you demonstrate that you're listening to her if she's tossing around ideas?

* * * * * *

Points to Remember:

• **Darkest Secret #17: People hire the ones they're comfortable with. Even if you're the most qualified, that does not insure you will get the part.**

• **Your Countermeasure:**

Learn to observe what form of personality style the casting decision-maker has. Then rehearse to "put your best foot forward" (that is, avoid saying something that makes the other person uncomfortable).

•

CHAPTER 18
DARKEST SECRET #18: NOBODY CARES ABOUT YOUR FEELINGS OR IF YOU'RE TIRED. YOU'RE SUPPOSED TO PERFORM WHENEVER IN PUBLIC (THAT INCLUDES INTERVIEWS).

The paparazzi make their living in catching celebrities in candid (read embarrassing) moments. The hard truth is: everybody's watching and the actor must take special care to be civil and well-spoken, especially about colleagues in the business.

For example, Helen Hunt (Oscar winner, *As Good As It Gets*) demonstrates poise in interviews. Director Nancy Meyers, who cast Helen in *What Women Want*, said: "Helen is an original. A role model for what women can be—strong, sure of herself and sensitive. It's because of Helen's innate strength and intelligence that I wanted her for the part of Darcy. I thought it would be fun and challenging to get inside her head."

Helen Hunt had kind words for Nancy, too: "The great thing about Nancy was that she is absolutely in love with the

Tracy/Hepburn movies, so there was a classic feel to our movie. That meant it was smart and well-thought out. And the relationships between every character in the movie are funny and real, too."

We learn from Helen important attributes of successful actors: 1) develop your style and 2) be gracious toward your co-workers in person and in print (or video interviews).

Energize Yourself if You Don't Feel Like Going to the Audition

A successful actor takes care of herself. She exercises so she feels power coursing through her veins. For example, Emilio Estevez and Tom Cruise run together down city streets. Emilio said, "We don't worry about [the fans] because they can't catch us!"

What the Director is Thinking (about the Actor's energy level)

Directors are concerned with getting excellent performances from actors. Filming days are often sixteen hours long. A director counts on the actor to keep up his own energy level. When an actor comes into an audition, the director observes the actor for "clues." Based on these observations, the director may think, "This actor looks tired. Will he be tired on my set? Does he give all of his energy away at a party the night before? Will he be demanding since he looks like someone who doesn't take care of himself?" It's important to demonstrate that you are awake and alive. First impressions last.

Increase Your Energy with The 4 M's

Any time you feel tired, consider using one of these techniques, which I call The 4 M's: Mind, Music, Movement, and Meals.

1. Mind

Your mind can lead your body. Thoughts bring about feelings. Perhaps you've heard someone say, "You should think positively." So how do we do that? I use a method that I call the SwitchPhrase. These are words that shift my train of thought into a positive direction. When I have made a mistake and found myself dwelling on the pain, I have used a phrase to help me move on. This phrase is: I can do better.

When I repeat I can do better in my mind, I start focusing on how I can do better and that I have another chance to do better. Here's another example. On Sunday, Diane finds herself feeling anxious about her in-box waiting for her Monday morning. So Diane repeats Now to herself so that she stays in the moment and enjoys whatever she is doing on Sunday.

Now it's your turn. Pull out your personal journal and write some possible SwitchPhrases that will help shift the direction of your thoughts.

2. Music

Music relaxes. Music energizes. It turns the direction of our thoughts and feelings. In your personal journal, note musical pieces (or songs) that relax or energize you.

3. Movement

Move your body, and your body develops capacity. Some people enjoy dancing; others prefer Tai Chi. You feel stronger and you enhance your health. To get yourself in a more energized mood, you can begin with a 10-minute session on a stationary bicycle (for example).

Now make a plan. Use your day planner and record two physical activities you enjoy. What physical activity have you not done in years but would like to?

Exercise gets you in touch with "your instrument"—your body. Directors and producers often like actors who are graceful. For example, Harry Saltzman and Albert R. Broccoli, the original producers of the James Bond films, cast Sean Connery because they appreciated how he was a big, tough-looking man who still moved gracefully, specifically "like a cat."

Peace-creating Movement: Breathing and Meditation

When we breathe, we move our chest and our diaphragm. Here is a three-stage process to create peaceful energy:

Stage 1:

a) Tense your feet for five seconds and then let go of the tension while saying in your mind an affirmation like "Spirit relaxes my feet...." or "God relaxes my feet."

b) Go up your body...tensing and relaxing calves, thighs, buttocks, stomach, chest, arms, back, neck, face, and scalp. Keep saying an affirmation in your mind as you go along: "Spirit relaxes my feet. Spirit relaxes my calves . . ."

Stage 2 (Affirm-Breathing):

a) Breathe in deeply through your nose. As you do this, say a four-second affirmation like "Spirit fills ____(your first name) with peace.....or Love relaxes ____(your name)." As you breathe, let your stomach area expand. This allows your diaphragm to gently

expand.

b) Hold your breath for the duration it takes to repeat your four second affirmation.

c) Breathe out through your mouth (while you repeat your affirmation in your mind twice).

d) You can build up the length of time from four seconds to twelve seconds – gradually.

Stage 3:

a) You meditate by...

1) just observing your breath flow in and out gently

OR

2) concentrating on a word or phrase. You repeat the phrase in your mind, and that helps you let other, distracting thoughts flow by as if they are leaves on a stream of water.

You can do the meditation practice for six minutes, 15 minutes or more. Some experts recommend 30 minutes in the morning and 30 minutes at night. Only a few people do that. You'll notice that sometime during your meditation period, you will think of nothing. Time flies by. You want this time of silence or "space between thoughts." This process gives you the experience of profound peace.

4. Meals

Nutrition is key to overall health. Research reveals that stress depletes our bodies of vitamins like B-complex. Eat well, feel well, do well. Consult doctors, nutritionists, and textbooks for more information. In your personal journal, note the nutritious foods and vitamin supplements you need to add to your daily routine.

The Fifth "M"—Mighty Companions

You also need Mighty Companions, those friends who believe in you and who have an optimistic-realist approach.

The optimist makes sure to be busy training to be ready for opportunities. The optimist also goes out and "knocks on doors" to create opportunities. This takes a lot of energy, and many of us recover energy through loving and fun interactions with positive friends and supporters. Bette Davis said that her favorite song was "Someone To Watch Over Me." To be a working actor who has the endurance to go the long haul, you need to develop and maintain a circle of friends.

* * * * * *

Make Time for Yourself to Feel Refreshed Before the Audition

Some years ago, Robin Williams was asked by an interviewer if he's "always on." Robin replied, "My son says, "Daddy, sit. Daddy. SIT!" The conversation continued, and Robin implied that he switches gears—even if his child needed to enforce it. A successful actor takes care of herself. She makes sure that she feels refreshed before the audition. An actor needs to be 'at the top of her game.' The way to be in top form is to condition yourself for peak performance. Consider the elements of healthy living: exercise, relaxation, meditation, and excellent nutrition.

People in the industry say that Steve Martin is a quiet person when he is not performing on stage, movie screen or television. Steve began in stand-up comedy in 1964 and became extremely successful in 1976. He certainly knows how to persist. Steve said, "It's the lucky break but you're creating the lucky break."

Steve looks relaxed when he is performing. To make this happen, he always comes in for the week before he has an appearance on Saturday Night Live, the television show.

Steve noted, "David Mamet said, 'No art can come from the conscious mind.' [which means] once it comes from the conscious mind it's dead. You need to let it breathe and really come from your soul." To let art breathe, Steve focuses on rehearsal. He rehearses so much that he feels relaxed and has the freedom for the performance to flow from his soul.

Rehearsal requires energy, and energy comes from the elements of healthy living: exercise, relaxation, meditation (or quiet time), and excellent nutrition.

What the Director is Thinking (about Actors making sure they're refreshed before the audition)

Action directors need actors who take care of themselves physically and emotionally. When I run an audition, I look carefully to see if the actor is physically fit and energetic. I need to count on the timing of the action-actor—to ensure safety on the set.

You need to keep yourself refreshed because you may need to wait a long time before you get your few minutes to audition. For the first Harry Potter film (and the rest of the eight- film series), Emma Watson (who portrays "Hermione Granger") was one of the last two girls to audition for the role. Although she may have waited all day, Emma had to express energy and flexibility during her audition.

During an audition, I look for actors who have a pleasant disposition. I listen carefully to their conversation patterns. Are they complaining? There is a big difference between complainers and solution finders.

I appreciate solution finders and welcome people to tell me about items that need correction. When I have worked with a complainer, I have also asked the person to inform me about errors in a private discussion. I emphasize that I want my set to be harmonious and a good environment for creative risk-taking. I also take careful note of what actors say in print. The crucial point is that the successful actor keeps up her own morale. And she vents her negative feelings off the set—and not in print—with a friend or a therapist if necessary.

Here are methods to help you take care yourself and then come to an audition feeling refreshed.

1. Combine activities.

If you need to return phone calls to friends, you can ride a stationary bicycle and call at the same time. You can watch a favorite TV program and ride your bicycle at the same time. In your personal journal, note activities you can combine to get double value for your time.

2. Say, "no, thank you" effectively.

Here are some notes on saying "no" without hurting the other person's feelings. This is a complicated issue. The words we use vary, depending on our personal style, the other person's style, and the situation in the moment. Here are some ideas you can use:

1) *Take care of your own feelings, and you will have the energy to be good to others.*

My coaching clients have mentioned how they eventually "lash out" with irritable remarks when they have gone through a period of accommodating others too much—and ignoring themselves. So we have a choice: a) say "no" at times, or b) erupt like a volcano later. You can say, "I'll have to say 'no' this time. My plate is full at the moment. I'm making sure I don't get overwhelmed...."

2) *Remind yourself that your saying "no" does not cause someone to feel hurt.* It just sets up a situation for the person to choose her reaction. Ultimately, it's up to her when she decides to move on. When you feel that you need to say no (in order to say 'yes' to yourself or something else), you can choose to help the other person to have a more positive reaction—if possible. (Unfortunately, some people stay stuck in their hurt for a while.) You can say, "I'm sad that I can't help this time. Maybe we can brainstorm here for a moment. Who do you know, who might be able to help with that?"

3) *Remember your first responsibility is to yourself.* I remember one time I was vacationing with a friend. He chose to wait for me and not to eat breakfast. I had a number of time-urgent tasks (checking in with my office) to do that morning. Later, he was upset because he was feeling pangs of hunger. Part of my response was, "I'm sad that you feel uncomfortable. Please do what you need to do to feel comfortable." So we planned to go our separate ways, then meet up later. When interacting with adults, we all feel better when we create a space for people to take care of personal needs.

4) *Stay open to accepting your uncomfortable feelings around saying "no."* In the above "breakfast example," my first response was to feel bad that my friend was hurting. I said, "Please do what you need to do to feel comfortable," to remind myself that his decision was his own.

How you can effectively say "no":

a) Learn to say "no" graciously. You can say, "Thank you for asking.... Thank you for thinking of me...."

b) Say "no" as soon as possible to give the other person

notice.

c) Acknowledge the other person's feelings.

d) Acknowledge any errors you may have made: like not calling back sooner.

e) Decide if you want to help the person look for alternatives.

f) Accept the times when the other person stays stuck in a hurt mood.

g) Decide if it is appropriate to "make it up" to the person— Perhaps with a small gift.

h) Stay open to accepting your own uncomfortable feelings around saying "no."

i) Stay in contact with the person. You may decide to let the person "cool off" for a day or more, then touch base with them.

The above ideas are like a menu. Try some of them and see what works for you. From a spiritual point of view, it helps when we remember: "My Spirit is bigger than my current uncomfortable feelings. I can choose to focus on my Spirit." [More spiritual ideas are found in my book *10 Seconds to Wealth: Master the Moment Using Your Divine Gifts*.]

3. Trade tasks.

Often, we can get more done when we trade tasks with a friend. And in this way, we can reserve more energy for the next audition. One time, I helped a friend by typing up his term paper. Since I typed over 73 words a minute, that saved him time. He helped me with editing for one of my projects.

Now, take out your personal journal and note two friends and two tasks that you can trade with them.

4. Invest in help.

People often say that they don't have the money to hire any help. Sometimes, we can shift a personal budget. For example, if you avoided two morning lattes, you might be able to hire someone for minimum wage to help with the gardening. You might consider hiring a high school student who is a member of the computer club to do your actor's website instead of devoting hours to learning how to make a website on your own. We can make more money, but we cannot replace the time of our life. In your personal journal, note tasks you'd like to assign for getting some low-cost help.

Points to Remember:

- **Darkest Secret #18: Nobody cares about your feelings or if you're tired. You're supposed to perform whenever in public (that includes interviews).**

- **Your Countermeasure:**

Use the Five "M's" (Mind, Music, Movement, Meals and Mighty Companions) to energize before the audition (or anytime you're in public—including interviews).

CHAPTER 19
DARKEST SECRET #19: MANY TIMES, THE BEST NETWORKERS, MEETING CASTING DECISION-MAKERS OUTSIDE OF AUDITION ROOMS, WORK MORE THAN THE BEST ACTORS.

Successful actors often meet decision-makers outside the audition room. A positive first impression at a networking event can pave the way for a warm reception during an audition. A dramatic example of meeting someone outside the audition room occurred when Producer David O. Selznick stood watching the 'burning of Atlanta' set on the backlot—for his production, *Gone With The Wind*. By the fiery glow, David had his first glimpse of Vivian Leigh—as his brother said, "David, meet your Scarlett O'Hara!"

Roy Scheider got a leading role in major blockbuster feature film because he met a film director at a party. Here's how Steven Spielberg later described what happened:

"I was at a party at Andre Eastman's house and I met Roy Scheider for the first time. He walked over to me and I was literally sitting on a couch with a Coca-Cola in my hand fretting over *Jaws*, that I wasn't able to get this shark movie cast, and Roy sat down and introduced himself. Of course, I had loved him so much in *The French Connection* and then in *The Seven Ups*. Roy actually said to me, "You have such a glum look on your face. What's the matter?" I said, "Aw, I'm having trouble casting my picture." He actually said, "Who have you gone out to?" I named a few names and he looked at me and said, "What about me?!?" He actually said, "What about ME?!?" in only the way Roy could do that, with his voice kind of cracking the way it does when he hits that high note. I looked at him and said, "You're right! What about you? Will you make my movie?" Without even asking for a script he said, "Of course! If you want me, I'll do it!" And we actually agreed at a party that he would play [Chief] Brody [in *Jaws*]… that night… at Andre Eastman's house. And then he read the script and loved it, which was good because he could have read the script and thrown it back in my face. But he loved it."

What the Director is Thinking (about Meeting Me Outside the Audition Room)

Observing actors at industry events, directors consider: "Does this actor carry himself with poise? Will he be an asset to promoting the picture through talk shows and interviews?"

Recently, it became clear to me what a successful actor has . . . a brand! Some actors have the brand "leading actor." Others have the brand "reliable character actor/actress." But there is another level to the "branding process." It's trust. Can the director trust that she will be able to get what she needs from a particular actor, without a bunch of needless trouble? Steve Jobs said, "To me a brand is one simple thing, and that is trust."

At a screening of another director's feature film, I was talking with an actor. When I asked if he had a business card, he gently asked if I'd like a copy of his headshot. I said, "Yes." I still remember him about five years later; his first name is Steven.

I often have the opportunity to interview top professionals. During my interview with Susan RoAne, best-selling author of *How to Work A Room,* I asked, "Knowing what you know now, what would you have done differently?" She replied, "Knowing what I know now about the publishing industry, I would have tripled my fees when my book appeared in *USA Today* and the *Wall Street Journal.*"

As an author and speaker, I have tucked away that tidbit of advice. And then I thought about Susan RoAne's other advice in her role as a mingling expert. What is a mingling expert? She coaches clients and audiences in ways to make the most of networking opportunities.

Five Methods from Top Mingling and Networking Experts

1. Ask

Patricia Fripp, one of the top speakers in the country, and author of *Get What You Want,* says, "The answer is always 'no,' unless you ask."

So if we want help, we need to ask. Perhaps you'd like the host/hostess to introduce you to someone; you can ask. In your personal journal, note what you can ask for that will make your dreams come true.

2. Use the methods of professional listeners.

Susan RoAne, in her book *What Do I Say Next?,* advises us

to use the methods of professional listeners. A professional listener includes anyone who responds to the needs of a client. Such listeners also include top salespeople who make their living by creating rapport with many people. Their methods include:

a) Eye contact
b) Slight nodding
c) Focus on us and our words
d) Questions and comments
e) Hearing even what [people] don't say!

"Hearing what people don't say" is about listening for the real meaning between the lines. A good listener also really watches body language. If a person says, "I like that actor" but her mouth is downturned in a slight frown, she may be giving away her actual distaste for that person.

In your personal journal, note the above listening skills you feel you need to practice. Then use your day planner and phone and seek to rehearse with a friend.

3. Remember interesting events and add them to your conversations.

Susan RoAne invites us to remember interesting events, moments, and stories with this process:

"1. Focus on what you just saw and heard. Review it in your mind.

2. Write it down! Humorist Jeanne Robertson keeps 'Jeanne's Journal.' These are not jokes or 'borrowed' stories. They are her observations and incidents collected from cab drivers, bell staff, clients, etc. She writes them down so she knows she won't forget them!

3. Read your notes.

4. Practice telling these stories to friends, relatives, and the

mirror."*

* from Susan RoAne's book, *What Do I Say Next?*

In your personal journal, write a rough draft of an interesting event from your life.

4. Practice the methods of the leaders who are "great talkers."

Susan RoAne has written the following methods that great talkers use:

"a) Honor people's time. Be bright, be brief, be gone. [You can follow-up your conversation with a brief email message.]

b) Smile and use humor.

c) Tell amusing or engaging anecdotes.

d) Listen, observe, study.

e) Relax, share, and have faith.

f) Engage in eye contact.

g) Enjoy life and others will find you enjoyable.

h) Remember that everyone has something to share. Conversation is fun, stimulating and educational.

i) Be courteous.*

* from Susan RoAne's book entitled *What Do I Say Next?*

In your personal journal, note methods you want to use during the next networking event you attend.

5. Be seen.

Patricia Fripp, in her book *Get What You Want,* notes that she receives so much media and press attention because for fifteen years she has been actively promoting herself. She says, "I have received many requests for speaking engagements from people who have read one of my articles– a perfect example of how the 'spider web' works. The spider-web concept involves doing things, being active, getting out there and being visible in your community–not just for a payoff but as a way of life."

We can apply Patricia's spider-web concept to networking for a great acting role in this way: be active and often your reputation will precede you.

In your personal journal answer the following questions: How can you be more active in the community? How can you meet more people? What is important to you? Perhaps you can apply to a local association and volunteer your efforts.

A number of actors meet studio personnel at charity events.

Points to Remember:

- **Darkest Secret #19: Many times, the best networkers, meeting casting decision-makers outside of audition rooms, work more than the best actors.**

- **Your Countermeasure:**

Use methods of professional listeners (ask good follow-up questions) and "great talkers" (prepare your anecdotes and engage in eye contact).

CHAPTER 20
DARKEST SECRET #20: HOLLYWOOD PEOPLE ARE SUPER-BUSY AND THEY RESENT NEOPHYTES CAUSING THEM PROBLEMS OR WASTING THEIR TIME.

Terms You Must Know and Professional Actions to Do

On the set, you must know the first three terms noted below. In addition, I have included the other terms because production personnel on the set will be talking about these items.

Term #1: Position One

Position One is the first place you stand just before the camera starts rolling. For example, Sabrina stands to the far right outside of the shot. When "Action!" is called, Sabrina walks across the screen to the left. The position to the far right is Position One for Sabrina.

Term #2: Return to One

The Assistant Director says, "Return to One" when she

wants people to return to their individual Position One.

Term #3: Reset

The Assistant Director says, "Reset," when she wants everyone to return to Position One, and this request also calls for the camera crew to return to their original position.

Term #4: Slate

To slate is to say your name and agent before you do anything else on camera. As an actor, I have auditioned for commercials in which a video camera is trained on me and I slate (say my name and agent) and then turn right and left for my profiles. If you do not have an agent, you can just say your name. Some acting coaches suggest that you go into character as you say the slate. Why? You are making the first impression. For example, if you are auditioning for a Klingon (Star Trek) you might say something like:

"Qapla! My name is Mark Smythe also know as Commander Korath. My human agent is Sam Jerston." [Qapla is pronounced "k-PLAH"—if you were curious.]

Term #5: Monologue

To do a monologue is to perform a two to three-minute dramatic work in which only your character is talking. It is important to ask, "Where do I play to? Over there or to you?" It is better if the director allows you to play to an imaginary person. You then choose a point near the director so she can see your face. But you must be ready for the director who says, "Play to me."

Term #6: Demo video

After performing in a few productions, you can put together a demonstration video known as a demo video or reel. Or, as we discuss in the later section *BOOK II: Taking Control of Your Career: Producing Your Own Short Film, Feature Film or Web Series,* you can produce a short film featuring yourself in the type of role you wish to audition for. Making your own short film puts your career in your own hands: a) you improve as an actor and b) you produce footage that can be your first demo video. Having control of your own footage solves the problem of waiting to get footage from filmmakers for whom you've worked. Make sure to have your photo and contact information on the disc and the case. Be prepared also to have copies that have your photo and only your agent's contact information for those times when your agent is sending out your material.

Term #7: Improv and Improvise

Directors, like myself, want to see the natural energy of actors come across on the screen. During an audition I will have actors make things up in the moment, that is, improvise.

During one audition, I saw a child who was good only when she was focused on the prepared script. I was concerned that she would be unable to respond to the spontaneous ideas that happen on a set. She did not get the part.

Practice improvising. On feature film sets, actors are often called to improvise. Many terrific lines in feature films have been improvised by the actors. A prime example is the line in *Jaws,* spoken by Roy Scheider as Chief Brody: "You're gonna need a bigger boat."

Another example: for the Parisian scenes of *Casablanca,* Humphrey Bogart ad-libbed the line "Here's looking at you, kid." This played so well that it was added to a later scene of the film.

Term #8: Casting Director

The casting director is hired by the production company to select potential actors. The director or producer makes the decisions. For a number of productions, a casting director saved me many hours because I only see twenty people (she prescreened) while she is in contact with thousands.

Term #9: Agent (agency)

An agency represents you to the agency's clients. The agency gets a percentage of the acting fee received from the agency's client. Here's an example. An agency's client, an advertising company, develops a television commercial. Then the company hires the agency to locate the actors for the commercial.

Requirements to Be Professional:

1. Check your cell phone messages often.

Casting decision-makers must be able to reach you quickly, and you must return their calls quickly. Often, the race goes to the person who responds the soonest. Even if you do not know the answer, it helps to reply quickly with something like: "Marina, I got your message. I'm very interested in the role of Susan Avegard. I'm looking to move some things so I can be at the audition on Wednesday afternoon. I'll call back soon with confirmation."

2. Repeatedly check email/text messages, Facebook, and LinkedIn.com (and any other networking system you use).

Sometimes, actors surprise me with how slow they are in replying to messages.

I personally take the opposite approach. While writing this book, one of my contacts informed me that she knew a casting director who needed someone matching my description to portray a doctor for a project. Within fifteen minutes, I was leaving a voicemail for the casting director. Within 24 hours, the role was mine. There are plenty of Asian middle-aged performers, but I got the role because I respond fast!

If you're using Facebook and LinkedIn.com (or some other social media website) be sure to check the message in-box at least once a day. It helps to use the function on Facebook or LinkedIn.com that pings you in your primary email account.

Let me share with you how crucial it is to respond quickly. My company often hires interns and contractors. The applicants who do not respond quickly fail to get an internship or contract. If an intern also proves to be slow in responding to voicemail or email, he is likely to lose chances to get subsequent contract work.

3. Use a contact management program.

Be sure to stay in touch with your important contacts by using a contact management software program. Every time you interact with someone, you can note what transpired. You want to be careful about sending information twice (like a postcard) and you want to avoid pestering people with too many email or phone calls in a short time span.

4. Keep your own morale up; handle rejection with a Did Well/Area to Improve Diary.

I mentioned the "Did Well/Area to Improve" Diary elsewhere in this book, and it bears repeating here. After an audition, you can write something like:

"January 17th. I DID WELL: looked the person in the eyes

Area to Improve: forgot to talk about my karate class."

The beauty of this system is that after you make the entry, you can close your diary and move on to something else in your day. This can help if you've ever obsessed over the audition during other parts of the day. When you write down what you've learned, you can feel better about the situation.

Diaries are helpful. Before she was a star, Marilyn Monroe wrote in her diary, "I won't worry about all the other girls. I'm dreaming the hardest." She persisted!

It is important to realize:

a) Sometimes, a person goes through twenty auditions or forty auditions until there is a match.

b) Many great things take a lot of effort (examples: 130 rejections before *Chicken Soup for the Soul* found a publisher; 22 rejections before the science fiction novel *Dune* found a publisher).

c) Every audition is an opportunity to learn something or practice for the next audition.

d) We learn by doing. If something is not working, change your approach and strategies—and get help (a coach, books, etc.). After each audition, write an entry into your Did Well/Area to Improve Diary.

5. Enhance Your Own Self-Esteem: Have Effort-Goals and Results-Goals.

We can always feel good about ourselves when we take appropriate action.

On the other hand, results are out of our hands. Be clear about the difference between efforts and results. Let's focus on this metaphor: "Keep swinging the bat, and eventually you'll hit the ball!"

I coach my clients and audience members to list two different forms of goals: a) Effort-goals and b) Result-goals.

Set up Effort-goals like sending email to all of your contacts. It is important to have Result-goals such as five roles in the next four months. Then you can ask yourself, "How can I make that happen?" Finally, set up Effort-goals such as: two phone calls a day and three emails a day. And it is crucial to be good to yourself and celebrate each step forward you take. Reward yourself when you complete an effort-goal.

Points to Remember:

- **Darkest Secret #20: Hollywood people are super-busy and they resent neophytes causing them problems or wasting their time.**

- **Your Countermeasure:**

Study and memorize the terms that professional actors need to know. Make sure that you respond quickly and in a professional manner to any voicemail, email, or text message.

CHAPTER 21
DARKEST SECRET #21: STUNT CHOREOGRAPHERS DO THEIR BEST TO KEEP ACTORS SAFE, BUT EACH ACTOR MUST LOOK OUT FOR HIS OR HER PERSONAL SAFETY.

In any action film, safety needs to come first. The blockbuster film *Titanic* had huge, complicated scenes. During a chat interview, director James Cameron took a lighthearted question: "Mr. Cameron, were all the extras accounted for at the end of the movie?" Cameron laughed out loud and replied, "In any endeavor this large, you have to expect losses." After smiling, Cameron said in all seriousness, "No one was ever reported missing. We had very complex safeguards against people being injured in the water. We utilized a buddy system and had a headcount after every take. It's important, sometimes we had 200 people in the water. There were also 30 lifeguards wearing costumes interspersed amongst the extras and stunt people."*

* from a chat interview on Online Tonight

When you work on any film, make sure you know what safety measures are in place; and take advantage of those safety measures. For example, if I had been an extra for Titanic, I would have positioned myself near a lifeguard (if possible). Upon hearing that there were lifeguards, I would have asked everyone near me to confirm whether she or he was a lifeguard.

You need to watch out for your own safety. Even when working with top stunt choreographers, actors get hurt. For Steven Spielberg's film, *Raiders of the Lost Ark,* Harrison Ford was actually dragged behind the truck for some shots. His ribs were badly bruised. The "making of the movie" crew asked Harrison, "Are you worried?" Harrison replied, "No. If it really was dangerous, they would have filmed more of the movie first."

For *The Godfather,* James Caan was rigged with special effects equipment for the execution scene of his character Sonny. This scene cost $100,000, which was a large figure for 1971. Caan was rigged with dozens of explosive squibs. A squib is a little explosive pack with movie blood. Caan was rigged with more squibs than had been ever attached to a person up to that time. Electric wires to activate the squibs (little explosive packs with movie blood) led down his back, through his left pant leg, and into a firing console. Eight face hits or small plastic blisters filled with movie blood were attached to his face. Extremely thin fishing line would pull the blisters apart, causing the blood to flow down his face.

A technician told Caan, "I've never put this many squibs on a guy in my life." James replied, "I don't think it was necessary for you to tell me that now."

When Francis Ford Coppola said, "Action," the squibs

exploded, the face hits flowed, and James writhed in simulated agony as Sonny and his car were strafed by machine gun bullets. The scene worked perfectly.

Actors may be advised to close their eyes when the face hits are activated in case the fishing line breaks by accident. Regardless, as an actor, you must watch out for your own safety.

What the Director is Thinking (about Safety on the set)

During my workshops, I tell the participants, "Never assume that your colleague is sane!" You must take personal care for your own safety. For example, for one of my feature films, I held onto the hood of a speeding classic Chevy truck—by my fingertips. Now I would have expected that the stunt driver would have driven as slowly as possible.

If I was the driver, I would have asked, "Can I go 20 miles an hour?" Well, I was surprised when the stunt driver gunned the engine and raced the truck down the road at 60 miles an hour! I felt every bump of the road, and I realized that I could be bounced off this truck and roll under the front wheels!

The speeding driver had caught what I call *Filmmaking Fever*—that's when people will take incredible risks just to get a good shot. It's a form of temporary insanity. Watch out that you don't catch it yourself. For one feature film, the scene called for my character to dangle from the top of a cliff, hands clinging to the banister of a staircase. There were two ways to film the shot: safely with a bit of movie magic–or dangerously. My adrenaline was pumping, and as the director, I could do anything. The safe way was for me to hang from the lower section of the stairway with the camera pointing skyward. I would only be six feet up in the air – above the sand of the beach.

The dangerous way was for me to go to the top of the cliff and dangle from the portion of the stairway up there. Thank goodness my rational mind overruled my filmmaking fever-emotions! I realized that I had no idea whether or not the banister at the top of the

staircase was sturdy enough to support my weight. My team had not built the staircase for a stunt. Even if the banister seemed sturdy enough at first, right in the middle of the shot, it could have broken away.

A second time I overruled filmmaking fever was during the filming of another feature film. I was filming at a home in San Rafael, California. I decided a high-angle shot would be great for a scene. My cameraperson immediately volunteered to climb on the roof and get the shot. I preferred to take the risk myself. So I had a stand-in take over my role and wear my character's clothing. I climbed up a rickety ladder, strained and barely pulled myself onto the roof. Then the crew handed the camera up to me. After filming the shot with the double portraying my character, I prepared to descend from the roof. I discovered there was no safe way to get down. I would have to reach my foot down about six feet to the rickety ladder. There were no safe handholds—only a flimsy, plastic gutter for siphoning water off the roof. All I would accomplish would be to break the gutter and crash down onto the cement.

A member of the team suggested that we call the fire department. I took a deep breath and said, "Yes." I realized that I would do no good in risking a broken leg. I was scheduled for the next shots to be filmed that day. So I asked for some socks for my hands because the roof was hot as a frying pan. I used an umbrella so I wouldn't be cooked before my next shot. Collapsing from heat exhaustion was not an option. A crewperson handed up my lunch. Just as I began to eat, the very helpful fire department arrived. I appreciated their care and expertise. Oh, there was one fireman's comment about "Don't let him eat–and he'll come down like any cat."

Actors can easily catch filmmaking fever. A number of actors have famously done some of their own stunts. For example, Paul Newman did his own bicycle stunts *for Butch Cassidy and the Sundance Kid* when his stuntman could not stay on the bike.

Safety and a Major Stunt

In the motion picture *Maverick,* starring Mel Gibson and Jodie Foster, one stunt called for the Maverick character to leap from a stagecoach to the lead horses of a six-horse team, pulling the stagecoach. Stuntman Mic Rodgers said, "The only thing that can go wrong—catching the horses out of stride. No one ever catches them both out of stride."

The worst thing DID happen. Mic said, "Everything was moving, everything was fluid, and even with all our preparation, all our planning, when I made the final jump, I caught both lead horses off stride and knocked them down into the dirt. I watched the left leader put his nose into the dirt for about thirty feet. I was just waiting for the coach to land on me and for all of them to wad up underneath me. I thought that the coach was going to crush me and kill everybody—kill [stuntmen] Tommy and Mike and the doubles inside. This all went through my mind. I figured the only reason they didn't tip over was because the other four horses were pushing them. On the one hand I was terrified, on the other hand I was lovin' it. It is the most exciting thing I have ever done in my life."

Later, Mel Gibson did some of his own stunts. Mic Rodgers said, "For the close-up shots, we put Mel [Gibson] out there between the teams of horses with them going full speed. There is really no way to do that and be perfectly safe. The only assurance of safety is his own ability. Dick Donner [the director] was naturally concerned for Mel's well-being and asked if we could cable him on. You don't want Mel connected to these horses in case they stumble. Dick then asked if we could strap Mel's feet in, and we didn't want to do that either because if he slips, then he is going to be dragging underneath the hooves of six horses. Donner wanted to know what, if anything, we could do. I told him Mel is a smart guy, an intelligent man with a lot of heart. Show him how it works, what to do, what not to do, and let it roll. Mel can take care of his own business. He's always been that way. I can put Mel into a room of fire and say, 'Don't go left, don't go right, and you'll be fine. And if not, I'll come get you.' He has faith in me, he trusts me, and that makes a true team relationship."

Learn to work well as part of a team. For the big final fight scene of *Lethal Weapon IV* the team included Chinese action star Jet Li (star of more than 25 Asian action films), second-unit director Conrad Palmisano, stunt coordinator Mic Rodgers, and Corey Yuen (Li's long-time professional associate and fight coordinator). Producer Joel Silver calls the final fight "the ultimate martial-arts skills pitted against the shrewdest, most seasoned street fighting." The final part of the fight was filmed in a deep-water tank, into which Mel Gibson and Jet Li fall as their battle ends. The actors worked underwater with off-camera scuba divers, providing oxygen as needed. Mel Gibson said, "Riggs and Murtaugh may complain they're too old for this . . . but I have to admit that it was fun doing it all one more time."

In the 1990's professional stuntpeople went through 8,510 injuries on numerous sets. With that in mind, use the following methods to help you develop safe ways of working.

1. Listen first.

Often the person explaining something will become irritated if she is interrupted before she finishes talking. Therefore, listen first. Let her say what she needs to. If appropriate, you might ask, "Oh. Is there anything else I need to know?"–before you start talking.

2. Ask questions to ensure you understand; draw a picture.

The only dumb question is the one you do NOT ask when you need to. In addition, it helps when you say, "Let's think on paper." You can draw a sketch that reveals your understanding of the scene. This process gives all the participants one place to focus their attention. Often, as you draw the picture someone says, "Oh, but you forgot the part where Sam runs in …"

3. Ask questions to make sure your colleague understands the plan.

Actors in an action scene must rely on each other so that they both stay safe. I ran a particular audition and certain martial artists really hit each other during the audition—even after they were advised to avoid contact with the martial art movements. I did not hire them because I knew they would not protect the lead actor. To maintain safety on the set, it's important to ask your colleague gentle questions like: "Just so I know that I said this clearly, what did we just agree to?" or "I just want to make sure I understand the pattern. I throw a right punch and then you . . .?" You need to do this delicately. It does help if you let the other person finish the sentence you have started. Then you know from the other person's words that he or she knows his or her part in the choreography.

4. Have at least two backup plans, and rehearse for the possibility that something may go wrong.

Professionals have a plan B and a plan C. It is valuable to say to team members, "What if Sam isn't able to swing the car to the right? What should I do to compensate?"

5. Have a Personal Safety Escape Plan

When I directed one of my feature films, the scene called for me (as actor/stuntman) to land a jet ski into the flatbed of a pickup truck. My personal safety escape plan was to let go of the jet ski if things went astray. And things went wrong! During the first take, the jet ski and I missed the flatbed. I let go! Fortunately for both the jet ski and me—we landed in some mud.

Later, we filmed the scene. In the film, you can see me coming down into the flatbed. Look closely at my face. My eyebrows were furrowed in tension because I almost fell out of the flatbed—going at forty miles an hour. To ensure your safety, you must have a personal escape plan! Think ahead. Write down at least three things that can go wrong and what you will do to ensure your personal safety.

6. Do a "slow-motion run through."

For one fight scene, I worked with two actors. I had us walk through the scene as if it were a slow-motion sequence. One actor did a punch slowly, and I slowly ducked. The other actor slowly punched, and I simulated being hit. Only with a slow-motion run-through can everyone be sure that each team member clearly knows his or her task. [You can see one of my fight scenes on YouTube.com: "Red Shirt's Revenge Tom Marcoux" or go to http://bit.ly/13zCGfO]

7. Note a safety area for yourself.

In one fight scene, one actor was to punch toward my face. I set up the scene so that he punched straight forward. In this way, I knew that I had to keep my face out of a one-foot in diameter area—so that I would be safe even if he wavered or punched too soon. I took action to create my own safety area—a safe space for me to occupy.

8. Set up stunts for the physical skill set of the participants.

When I choreograph a fight scene, I study the individual characteristics and capabilities of each performer. For one of my films, I choreographed a fight scene in which my character defends his daughter from a gang of hoodlums. The actors were not stuntmen who do fight scenes every day. I know from experience that novice actors feel uncomfortable about falling backwards onto padding. There can be a slight hesitation which can spoil the scene. My solution is to have the actor simulate being hit so hard that it spins him around. So as the actor appears to take a kick across his face, he spins around and then falls out of the camera frame. Then he lands on his hands—on pads on the ground.

This process worked well because since they could see where they were falling they did not hesitate.

On the other hand, trained stunt people are ones who can safely land on their backs.

Points to Remember:

• **Darkest Secret #21: Stunt choreographers do their best to keep actors safe, but each actor must look out for his or her personal safety.**

• **Your Countermeasure:**
Note a "safety area" for yourself. For example, if you are in a fight scene, identify the area where you can keep your face safe from being accidentally hit. Ask for a slow motion run through of the stunt so you can double-check your understanding of the requirements. Remember that you must watch out for your own safety. The set is a hectic place, and you must make sure that potential human errors do not endanger your personal safety.

* * * * * *

Now that you know some elements of filmmaking, it's time to provide you with more information. In the next section, *BOOK II: Taking Control of Your Career: Producing Your Own Short Film, Feature Film or Web Series,* I provide you with methods so that you can produce a short film, feature film, or some demo video footage. Finally, you do not have to wait to be chosen for a role. You can cast yourself and get your Hollywood career moving forward.

BOOK II: TAKING CONTROL OF YOUR CAREER: PRODUCING YOUR OWN SHORT FILM, FEATURE FILM OR WEB SERIES

Do you need demo video footage? Are you waiting for someone to cast you in a role and you're getting frustrated? Here is the good news. You can take control of your career and produce a short film and cast yourself in the type of role you're aiming for. You could film a 30-second trailer for a proposed feature film and then use the footage for your demo reel. You could place this material on YouTube.com, which makes it easy for you to send a link to the video clip in email. You could hire a high school student; one of my colleagues did just that and had the student teach her details about YouTube.com. Soon she had him editing demo videos for her.

Many people took action and proved to Hollywood that they had talent. They didn't wait to be cast. They cast themselves. Actor Bruce Campbell began his career as a first-time producer working with first-time director Sam Raimi, who later directed the mega-hits *Spider-Man* and two sequels. Campbell and Raimi began with a low budget 16 mm feature film entitled *The Evil Dead*. Bruce was the lead in that film. Bruce went on to star in two sequels to *The Evil Dead* and secured roles in *Xena* and *Hercules* (the TV shows produced by Sam Raimi). You have probably heard of Sam Raimi, the director of the mega-hits *Spider-Man* and two sequels.

Bruce was the lead in a TV series entitled *The Adventures of Brisco County Jr.* He is currently co-starring on the hit TV series *Burn Notice.* The example of Bruce Campbell shows that it's possible to make your luck by being a producer, casting yourself in a feature film and showing Hollywood what you can do.

Billy Bob Thornton cast himself as "Karl," the lead of *Sling Blade,* and he also directed that feature film. He went on to have a significant role in the blockbuster Armageddon and many other films.

The present day is a fantastic time to be an actor because digital filmmaking opens so many doors. At the time of this writing, for only around a few thousand dollars a person can gather people and film an entire feature film. Often, independent filmmakers use deferred pay agreements with a clause that cast and crew will share in any profits from the commercial exploitation of the finished feature film. The independent filmmaker can purchase a home computer and editing software for a few thousand dollars. I know this for a fact because someone I know who makes a living as a bartender devotes his time to filming and editing his own digital feature films (four finished films so far).

Frustrated that he wasn't able to get good roles, Robert Townsend produced, directed and starred in his own film *Hollywood Shuffle* that sold to a studio for $3 million. He paid for the film with credit cards. How? He would use a credit card to purchase fuel for each actor's car, and in this way, he paid his actors. I am not recommending this method in particular. But I am saying that you can take matters into your own hands and make your dreams come true in some form.

You can also choose to produce your own demo film clip. I'll now share an example of the process.

a) Identify what acting roles you feel you would be ideal for.

b) Come up with a short film idea that showcase your talents. For example, I know a young man who would like to be seen as ideal for rookie cop roles. I wrote the premise for *Officer Down*, a 45-second film clip. Over the opening credits you hear: "And in other news, there have been a series of shootings of police officers in the __ area." As we hear this voiceover, we see a young, rookie police officer calling for backup. He then hears a woman scream and he enters the open door of a house. He walks through the house and many horrible Halloween decorations are in the foreground as he passes by them. We get the distinct impression that he is going to die and . . . . If this film clip is produced by the time this book goes to press, I'll include a link to YouTube.com. Otherwise, you still get the idea that you can demonstrate what roles you are ideal for by filming your own video clip.

This chapter includes a brief overview of specifics about digital filmmaking. Even if your heart tells you to avoid becoming a producer, it is still helpful for every actor to be aware of the filmmaker's process. Who knows? You might be able to make a closer connection with a director when talking about some details that you learn in this particular chapter.

Specific insights about Digital Filmmaking

1. Accommodate people who often view the material on a small screen.

Often, I view footage at YouTube.com and I don't click to enlarge the image. So when you film a video clip, be sure to include lots of close-ups. Wideshots on a computer screen or smart phone lack impact.

Secondly, use close-ups to create excitement. A number of filmmakers have said that the fight scene at the end of the feature film *Star Trek III* could have been more intense if there were more close-ups. Imagine a close-up of Captain Kirk's fist connecting with the Klingon's face. That creates impact.

2. Beware of a fragile sound jack.

Many DV cameras have a fragile sound jack. The sound jack is the socket where you plug the microphone cord into the camera. In fact, I know of a number of DV filmmakers who have lost good footage due to a sound jack failing. That person ends up with no sound for a full day of filming.

Overcome the potential problem of a faulty sound jack destroying your footage by having the microphone cord plug into a 'splitter' to send sound to the camera and to have sound go to a backup recording device.

Here's another solution. Use duct tape to hold up the microphone cord so that no weight of the cord places strain on the fragile sound jack. It is not a pretty solution, but it has worked for a number of filmmakers.

3. Take advantage of the ease of moving the small

digital camera.

A moving camera is used by many directors (including Steven Spielberg and Martin Scorsese) to pull the audience into the story. Because DV cameras are light weight, you can move the camera with great ease.

In addition, you can film in tight spaces. I directed a scene in which a character accidentally dropped a toothbrush into a toilet. I was able to get a low angle shot with the toilet in the foreground. No large size camera would have fit between the nearby bathtub and toilet.

You can film a chase scene with two characters running in an economical way. Borrow a wheelchair and invite the cameraperson to ride in the wheelchair. POOF—instant moving camera. *Warning:* Check your footage immediately by playing it back: some cameras are hypersensitive to jarring.

4. Use precise language on the set

Because you're using a smaller camera, actors and crew may feel that they're on an amateur set. To counteract that feeling, use precise language like:

Director: "Quiet on the set."

Assistant Director: "Quiet on the set."

Director: "Standby to roll camera."

Assistant Director: "Standby to roll camera."

Director: "Roll camera. Marker."

(an assistant snaps the clapperboard)

Director: "Action."

(the scene plays)

Director: "Cut."

This use of precise language can help actors get the magical feeling of "Yes, we're on a real set." Be sure to also snap the clapperboard (because if sound fails to reach the camera, you can sync-up your backup sound).

Some directors, including me, like to do an "end slate" on scenes involving strong emotion. That means one holds the clapperboard upside down and claps the board at the end of the scene. This helps protect the actor from the distracting Snap! sound of the clapperboard at the beginning of the scene.

For example, I directed a feature film scene in which a father "John" watched his brother take John's daughter out of a room. John's alcoholism was keeping him away from his daughter and the scene called for John's face to quake with emotion. This was an ideal situation to do an "end slate."

5. Prepare for actors who want immediate demo video footage

Since you are using video (and many video cameras have an on board hard drive), many of your actors will want an immediate copy. It is dangerous for a filmmaker to release footage that she may not even use in the final project. Many people in the industry view demo videos, and you do not to want make a bad first impression.

Here is a possible solution: you can use a software program like Final Cut or Adobe Premiere and place a subtitle on the footage like: "From the rough cut of the feature film, *One Rough Night*."

6. Consider FilmLook or a similar process.

Years ago, Jefferson Davis, the director of the feature film *The Ticket Out of Here* told me that he used Hi8 videotape, ran it through FilmLook, and had his videotape project accepted as a feature film at a major festival. Now, if FilmLook can make Hi8 videotape look great, then it can do much for more current digital video formats.

Allen Kelly of FilmLook Inc. had these words posted at filmlook.com: "So many producers and editors are working on laptops and they are doing everything right there—editing, sound design, and music," Allen says. "But, we find what looks great on your laptop sometimes does not meet broadcast standards and a distributor may not find it acceptable. As part of FilmLook's da Vinci 2K color enhancement service, we can assure that your projects will adhere closely to standards established by major networks and motion picture studios. Remember, most viewers will be seeing your work in a home environment on television, not necessarily just on a PC or laptop."

The Filmlook.com website continues with: "A great example of FilmLook's versatility is the A&E series 'Manhunters,' now in its third season. FilmLook has been doing the color enhancement on "Manhunters" since the pilot episode. The reality show follows U.S. Marshals who have the authority to pursue federal criminals across the country and around the world. The post production challenges are enormous, as there are sometimes three different camera crews working simultaneously. According to Allen, 'The different cameras have different color balances, the exposures are also different and vary from full daylight to night time surveillance, since it's run-and-gun, guerilla-style reality television. Of course, we need to match up the look and bring a consistency to the series.'"

The point is: the better your digital film looks, the more payment you can command from a distributor.

As a side note, the director of *The Ticket Out of Here* was later offered $2 million to reshoot his Hi8 video production on 35mm film. This is another example of how taking action today can lead to bigger opportunities in the future.

7. Take advantage of video playback.

Major directors use video assist, a system that allows filmmakers to view a video version of a take immediately after it is filmed. The directors view a playback of scenes as they shoot 35mm film or footage shot with a high-end digital video camera. Similarly, take advantage of your ability to play back the footage. When you work with a cameraperson who is new to you, check to see if your vision of a close-up is the same as the cameraperson's style of framing a shot. You can give your cameraperson immediate adjustments to make. When you are doing stunts, you can also find out immediately if you got the shot—and then, you can move on.

Also, if you're working with actors who are not trained for fight scenes, it is good to get the shot and not push them for too many takes. Actors who do not train every day run out of energy and are liable to make more mistakes and suffer injuries. Avoid this situation by viewing video playback and confirming if a first or second take has captured the magic you were aiming for.

8. Trust the camera's eyepiece over the display monitor.

When you are filming, trust what you see in the camera's eyepiece instead of the display monitor. Specifically, the edges of the image are not accurate on the display monitor. Our big concern here is the location of the boom microphone. Have you ever seen the boom mike in a film or television program scene? It can kick the viewer right out of the story.

When looking through the eyepiece, tell the boom operator to back away from the actor until you cannot see the boom. Then have the boom operator back away just a bit more. Also note that the eyepiece gives you a false impression of the frame edges in that a large screen television set will reveal more at the edge of the screen. That's why I invite you to have the boom operator back up for that "just a bit more."

9. Use non-linear editing to your advantage.

The old style of videotape editing was that you put in shot one, then attach shot two and so on. In non-linear editing, you place shots on a timeline, and you have massive flexibility in that you can move any shot anywhere. Use this to your advantage by placing your best shots first on the timeline. Then think about the transitions between shots.

In digital video: "performance is king." That means that the actors' performances are most important and good acting can elevate your film. An actor's performance can make or break the emotion you elicit from the audience. So start with the best takes and place them on the timeline.

The special advantage of placing your best shots on the timeline first is similar to the advantage that Disney Imagineers use when constructing an attraction for Disneyland. The Imagineers build a 3-D model of a new theme park ride. Then, they can and play with the elements—that is, move pieces around. Similarly, with non-linear editing, you can move things around and try new combinations in seconds. This saves time and frees your mind to explore many possibilities.

* * * * * *

How to Make Your Own Digital Feature Film

We'll now explore an overview of elements to help you ensure the quality of your own feature film—if you choose to produce one. Let's say that you are interviewing college students (and others) to find a film major who can best direct your project. If you interview "George" and he does not know what the 180-degree rule is (see Method #13 below), you realize that George is unlikely to know enough to direct your film well. Find someone with more expertise. As a side note, it is reported that Quentin Tarantino's first film (which was never completed) was unwatchable because he did *not* know the 180-degree rule. And so the actors did not look like they were talking to each other.

DEVELOP CONTENT

1. Use the fastest way to structure your digital film.

Use what I call "bookends." Begin your digital film with a startling image, and then end the film with the same image but with a significant alteration. For one project, I came up with the image of a young woman reaching for a knife for a suicide attempt, and at the end of the film, she reaches for a knife—and places grape jelly on a sandwich for her daughter. It is a happy ending because she did live to care for her baby.

2. Identify what a good publicity photo would look like.

Begin by drawing a couple of rough sketches to identify what a good publicity photo might look like. Why is this helpful? This process assists you to get to the heart of the film and how you're going to convey that essence to someone who sees a photo on a website or newspaper. Furthermore, when you focus on the essential image, you gain clarity in how to make write your digital film. In workshops, I say, "how you market it changes how you make it."

Here's an example of designing a publicity photo. I

designed a publicity photo that depicted two friends: one in a car and the other friend above him, clinging to the car roof. This photo showed the essence of the feature film: a) friendship, b) one friend is wacky and athletic, c) the other is tolerant, and d) the film has enjoyable humor and action. As you design the publicity photo, you may decide to add a scene to your screenplay.

3. Identify a scene you would display *on The Tonight Show.*

What scene from your film gives the viewer the essence of the film? What scene would you bring to the host to show on *The Tonight Show*? How would you explain the scene in response to the host's question: "Does this clip need to be set up?" This exercise helps you refine your film and helps you prepare for how you will present your film. You might want to film this scene first and then use it to show potential investors exactly what type of film you're making.

CAMERA

4. Use a "practical light."

When lighting a scene, use a "practical light," which is a light that would naturally be in the scene like a desk lamp.

5. Make good shots.

Here are important elements of good shot composition (described in the following methods):

- Have "look space." (Method #6)
- Avoid "natural cutting lines." (Method #9)
- Do not break the 180-degree rule. (Method #13)
- Use the z-axis when possible. (Method #14)

Another component of good shot composition is carefully

choosing the dominant element of the image. The dominant element of an image can be set by the relative size of the object. For example, you can place a baseball close to the camera lens and allow it to take up 50% of the image. And your composition could include a door in the background, through which an actor enters.

6. Use "look space."

When framing a shot, use look space, which is a portion of the screen that is in front of your subject's eyes that makes the shot aesthetically pleasing. In essence, you place the actor off center. You place more space in front of the actor.

7. Use "coverage."

Coverage is getting a number of camera angles so that you have sufficient "editing room." Use shots like: close-up, over-the-shoulder, two-shot, and long shot.

8. Use the Golden Mean.

The Golden Mean is an area of the camera frame that is slightly off center. Using the Golden Mean helps you make the shot aesthetically pleasing by providing "look space." With look space, you avoid the boring, merely centered shot.

9. Avoid conventional "natural cutting" places.

In framing a shot, a natural cutting place is a position on the body like: neck, waist, ankles, knees, center of the body, and under the nose. Avoid these natural cutting places because they make the shot look unprofessional and often make the shot look subtly disturbing. How? If you have a close up that cuts at the neckline it looks like the actor was decapitated. That's disturbing to most people—except for horror fans.

10. Use 3-point lighting for many shots.

You can accomplish 3-point lighting by using a key light, fill light and back light. The key light provides the brightest illumination on the side of the face that is facing the camera. The fill light softens the shadows on the other side of the face. The back light provides a golden outline on the hair to help the actor stand out from the background. Often, a dramatic scene can call for just one light. However, the 3-point lighting pattern is the standard process of the industry.

11. Have actors "cheat to the camera."

Cheating to the camera occurs when an actor turns her face toward the camera while still directing her eyes toward the other subject.

12. Use the screen direction of an actor's movement to tell the story.

The American cultural convention of screen direction includes: heroes walk left to right, and bad guys retreat to the left.

13. Use the "180-degree rule"

The 180-degree rule is a principle that helps the audience know where characters are in space. When you follow the 180-degree rule, you avoid having audience members getting confused.

For example, imagine seeing a quarterback throw a football to the right of the camera frame. But in the next angle the football is going in the opposite direction. This is easily solved by having all cameras on the same side of a football field.

Furthermore, the 180-degree rule helps you frame shots in a way that avoids the error of having actors appear to bounce from left to right (or the reverse) when camera angles are changed. The 180-degree rule also helps you avoid the error of an actor looking in the wrong direction during her close-up shot.

Following the 180-degree rule is also known as "keeping all cameras on the same side of the Action Axis." The Action Axis is the imaginary line that appears to go through the two subjects, which you cannot cross.

14. Use the Z-axis in your composition.

If you think of a graph, the x-axis and the y-axis can refer to width and height. The z-axis refers to depth. Here are the advantages of using the z-axis in the composition of your shot:

a) To make one component of the image more dominant.

b) To create a sensation of depth.

c) To make a more visually pleasing composition.

15. Use the power of a dolly-in shot.

Dollying in (rolling the camera closer to the subject) brings the viewer into the world of the character. Many directors, including me, find dollying in to be preferable to zooming in which brings the characters (like a photograph) toward the viewers.

16. Use a variety of shots.

Use the various shots: close up, medium, extreme close up, long, far, two shot, three shot, over the shoulder, cutaway, and insert shot. I prefer to use two cameras for the first take: one camera on a two shot to capture both characters and one camera capturing a close up of one character.

In addition, make sure to get an "over the shoulder" shot

for each character. On my set, we use a phrase like: "Get me an over the shoulder shot favoring Sam." The idea is that the shot is behind Janet's head so you can change Janet's dialogue (we cannot see her lips moving).

17. Use the convention about going from a trucking shot to an angle with a still camera.

The convention is to have the trucking (moving) shot stop before you cut to the angle using a still camera. If you cut from a moving camera to a still shot, it is like slamming on the brakes and jarring the audience.

18. Prepare for a decrease in depth of field.

Depth of Field refers to the area in which something is in focus. For example, if you were to film a line of people with person #1 near you and person #10 far away from you, the Depth of Field might be from person #1 to person #3.

Depth of Field decreases under low light conditions. This fact is especially important if you ever intend to use the automatic focus feature on your digital video camera. I tell my students to often avoid auto-focus. If you are shooting a "night scene" do NOT use auto-focus because the depth of field is so small that the focus constantly winks in and winks out as the DV camera struggles to find an object to focus on.

19. Use the POV camera angle.

POV means "point of view," and a POV camera angle makes the audience members feel that they're looking out of a character's eyes. This is especially effective if a character is walking through a house at night—and at any moment a knife-wielding villain can jump out of the darkness.

20. Be sure to do a "white balance" with your digital

video camera.

Please see the instruction manual for your particular digital video camera and look up "white balance." This process helps you set the camera so your subjects don't appear tinted orange. After you complete white balancing, you can more accurately photograph the subjects. As I say to my students, "It gets your whites whiter and your colors brighter."

SCRIPT WRITING:

21. Use various writing formats.

Here are the basics:

a) A step outline identifies each step. One notes the location and day/night, and a specific action that the character does. It would appear as: "1) INT. LIVING ROOM - DAY Joe puts a shoulder holster on and grabs his gun from a lock box."

b) A treatment is a present tense story version of the project (which can be five to 14 pages, typically).

c) A camera script includes specific camera directions and numbered scenes.

d) A story script uses "master scenes" and avoids both camera directions and numbered scenes. Filmmakers tend to provide story scripts for potential investors so that the story is *not* obscured by the jargon of "DISSOLVE TO, CRANE IN, etc."

AUDIO:

22. Prepare to troubleshoot if you cannot hear sound in your headphones

When filming, always have someone monitor the sound that is being recorded into the DV camcorder. It is also crucial that you play back the video recording to ensure the sound was recorded.

Here are typical reasons for the absence of sound:

a) Broken headphones
b) The mic switches are not on "mic."
c) The levels are not turned to "10"
d) The switch on your boom mic is not switched "on."
e) The microphone is broken.
f) There is a short in a cable.
g) A cable is unplugged.
h) Batteries are low.
j) Someone forgot to put the batteries in!

23. Create correct sound presence.

Sound presence refers to how we expect sound to have a certain texture. For example, a close-up shot will have the sound of the actor's mouth near the microphone. A far shot will also have more ambient sound. Correct sound presence is created by proper placement of the boom microphone.

24. Use minimal "A.D.R."

Automatic Dialogue Replacement (A.D.R.) is the process by which you replace sound recorded on the set with sound dubbed in a sound studio. A.D.R. can cause you significant problems: 1) it sounds artificial, 2) using a studio raises your budget, and 3) many actors either give a flat performance or have trouble with timing the words with the images. You can reduce A.D.R. by placing microphones nearer the actors, and avoid filming a dialogue scene next to consistent sounds like a pounding surf at the beach.

EDITING:

25. Correct a jump cut.

A jump cut is when the image "hops" because the editor

cut together two shots that are too similar. To avoid this situation, make sure that shots are at least 30% different—which means that a medium shot must be at least 30% bigger than a close-up. In editing, you can correct a jump cut situation by using a cutaway shot—that is, you can "cut away" to someone who is observing the main characters. Or you can use an insert shot, which can be a close-up of someone reaching for a can of soda, for example.

26: Use Alfred Hitchcock's distinction about the use of a close-up.

Alfred Hitchcock advised that a director orchestrate her shots and use the close-up like a "single musical instrument playing one note." The idea of "single instrument" is about focusing on one detail so much that it really dominates the moment for the audience.

27. Use deductive editing.

Deductive editing is the process in which the pieces add up in an analytical way. An example is: a) long shot of a building, b) medium shot of the hero approaching the door, and c) a close-up of the hero's hand turning the door knob.

28. Use an inductive editing style.

In inductive editing, the snippets add up to an impression or mood. The snippets do not need to proceed logically. For example, if I wanted to show how the main character feels overwhelmed by the busyness of her day, I could have a disjointed series of shots of "moments of her day" and I could use one shot over and over—like the chorus of a song. Perhaps that shot would be her mother's mouth berating her—to symbolize that her mind is obsessing over the point her mother made.

Here's another example. Some feature films have a sequence (like a music video) that shows a couple sharing time together: walking, shopping, smiling, having a lively conversation at a coffee shop, and more.

29. Use a match cut.

In editing, create a match cut by placing two shots next to one another and using the similarity of a visual element to make a smooth transition. For example, a match cut can start with a shot of the hero's hand lowering a telephone receiver; then the next shot is a foot lowering onto the sidewalk from a staircase. The match is related to the motion.

30. Use cutting on the action.

This form of editing relates to using a physical movement to make a smooth transition when the first camera angle is radically different from the second angle. For example, in one fight scene, I began with a two shot and then switched to a wider shot. This worked because I used the beginning of the kick in the first shot and then I used the foot connecting to the opponent's face in the second shot. So in essence, I "cut on the action."

DIRECTING AND WORKING WITH TALENT AND CREW:

31. When directing actors, use an "objective."

The director guides the actor to clarity with her objective, and thus improves the performance. One way to form an objective is: "I want _____ (verb) to this person so he/she does _____[verb]." Here's an example: "I want to convince George so he says, 'You're hired with a bonus.'"

SAVE TIME ON THE SET:

32. Use basic time-saving methods.

a) Tell people to arrive ½ hour early on the set before you need them.

b) Use a shot list.

c) Have storyboards.

d) Have your equipment set up before the talent arrives.

e) Foresee problems and have "plan B and plan C"—this is Gale Anne Hurd's phrase (She is the producer of *Terminator I, Tremors* and the TV series *The Walking Dead*).

f) Use set diagrams.

g) Give people enough advance notice and ensure that talent are prepared before they arrive on set.

h) Show your Director of Photography your storyboards.

i) Have paper and pencils to draw new storyboards at any time.

j) Delegate.

k) Rehearse.

l) Have a production meeting in the morning.

m) Standardize procedures and use precise language.

n) Help the actors give a great performance by helping them intensify their "objective."

TEAMWORK:

33. Use elements of teamwork.

An effective director inspires creative team members' commitment. The effective director listens first and makes an environment where feedback is welcomed.

34. Use elements of team leadership and synergy.

Sometimes directors and actors have a stand off. One solution is: "Commit to continue the dialogue until a synergistic solution is found." First, let's look at "synergy."

Synergy occurs when team members have a dialogue that includes different points of view and that creates a "third option" (unknown to either party before the dialogue). Synergy involves feedback.

For example, best-selling author Stephen Covey wrote about a situation when two coworkers shared an office. One person wanted the window open and the other wanted the window closed. A compromise would have left both people frustrated. The solution was to have the people continue a dialogue until a synergistic solution was found. People need to listen and discover useful details. The first person wanted the window open for the fresh air, and the other person wanted to avoid his papers flying about due to the breeze. The synergistic solution was to open a window in a nearby room.

Here is another example of synergy: on a film set, a director wanted a night scene lit rather bright—or so the director of photography (D.P.) thought. The D.P. wanted the scene with many dark areas so that the audience would feel that something could leap out at any moment. The director and D.P. continued their dialogue. The synergistic solution was for the D.P. to light a fence AND to let the background trees go dark. The surprising benefit was that two characters also cast their shadows on the fence on their way into the shot. That looked great!

Another form of synergy is titled "completed staff work." Napoleon had a three-step process:

a) His generals had to come up with three solutions to any problem.

b) Each general would need to choose one of the solutions, endorse it and explain his reasoning.

c) No general would come to Napoleon with a problem without first thinking it through.

A final idea related to synergy is about how people make decisions. Researchers note that people decide based on emotion and then support their decision based on facts. So

a D.P. can offer a lighting solution by first mentioning Alfred Hitchcock's style if she knows that the director has a special appreciation for Hitchcock's work. The director will probably go along with the lighting solution because his emotion would be engaged with the possibility of emulating Hitchcock.

35. Lead a team by providing for their needs.

Here are some basic methods:

a) Always have good craft services—food.

b) Listen first. That is, hear the person out.

c) Repeat what the team member has said (the exact words) so they know you heard and understood their meaning.

d) Ask "Did I get it? Is there anything else I need to know?"

e) In a team setting, avoid emphasizing who proposed an idea. Make it the group's idea. In this way, you can avoid ego clashes.

f) If you need to drop someone's idea, use a "straw person" (a fictional person). Here's an example: "I wonder how we would handle the situation if users [fictional] have difficulty with process AB?"

36. Use a "planning pattern."

In corporate video production, the producer handles these elements:

a) Budget

b) Deadline and schedule (milestones)

c) Client's desired outcomes

d) Client's concerns, expected challenges
e) Dealing with client's misperceptions and problems

If you're producing your own feature film (starring you!), you can think of yourself as the "client." You'll need help so that you can handle any misperceptions that you may have because this is your first feature film. A number of first-time directors have received help from veteran production team members when they approached them in a positive spirit. They have said, "This is my first feature. I'd appreciate your suggestions so I do better with this one."

My colleagues who work with corporate clients say that they have to educate the client as to the process of making a video production. In the same manner, you need to seek education in the form of books, mentors, and coaches, if you intend to produce your first feature film.

GENERAL:

The following methods are from my presentation "Using Audio and Video on the Internet: How to Do It Right!" which I gave at the National Association of Broadcasters Conference in Las Vegas, Nevada. During that presentation I used two acronyms: V.I.D.E.O. and A.U.D.I.O.

The next methods are based on the acronym V.I.D.E.O.

37. V - Visualize what you want the viewer to do immediately after viewing.

Your first digital video production may be a short film that you want for your demo reel and for your website. It is vital that you identify what you want the viewer to do immediately after viewing the video clip. Perhaps you want the viewer to immediately hire you for an action-feature film; then you'll want to have impressive fight scenes. At the end of the demo video, you can put the title: "Please call the number on this video." This is a good idea if you want your agent to send out copies of your video. Many agents do not want their contacts calling you directly.

Let's say you place your digital film on your website. You can put a comment at the end of your video:

a) "Please type in your email address to be informed about Janet Smygard's next live performance or film role."

b) "Please click on 'share with friends' to invite others to view this film. We're hoping that this film goes viral."

38. I - Involve the viewer with the *Power 3 Beginning*

As a faculty lecturer at Cogswell Polytechnical College in Silicon Valley, I taught my students powerful techniques in digital film production. Here are some items that their final exam covered: "For the beginning of your digital film, use one or more of these items: a) a dramatic question, b) a startling image and c) 'salting phrases.'"

Dramatic Question:

The first image must grab the viewer's interest and create the question: "What's going to happen?" For example, in my short film "Dimension Man," the first image is of the hero's face hitting the ground. Questions pop up in the mind of the viewer: "What happened - and what's he going to do about it?" or "Is he dead?"

Startling Image:

Wake up your viewer. She can easily change the channel or surf to another website or bounce to another film clip on YouTube.com.

"Salting Phrases"

This technique is based on the phrase: "You can lead a horse to water, but you can't make him drink—unless you salt his oats first." Maintain viewer interest by using strategic phrases like: "If I knew what was going to happen, I would have run the other way . . ." Or "No. I won't it let go. I'm going to make someone pay for the death of my father."

39. D - Devote time to structure, storyboards and Choice Market Testing.

With feature film writing, structure is crucial. The movie-going public has been conditioned to expect certain things to happen in certain sequences. Here are some brief details. The feature film is divided into the three-act structure. The first 10 pages are crucial; you need to introduce the quest and major characters. On the tenth page, something significant must happen. In my upcoming feature film *TimePulse,* a fight occurs during which the leading man arrives to assist the leading woman; and they meet each other for the first time.

Storyboards are sequential drawings that look similar to the images in a comic book. They are crucial for planning action scenes and special effects.

Choice Market Testing is a process I devised that helps you produce your film so it can appeal to your target market. For example, when you begin to pull your production together, you can have two sketches of your poster drawn up and then ask people, "Which movie would you pay to see?" You offer the person a choice; that's how I came up with the name "Choice Market Testing."

40. E - Earn the viewer's trust.

When you place your digital film on your own website, be sure that your website loads quickly. Website visitors are quick to become frustrated when kept waiting. Also, with make sure that the first shot of your film is startling or fascinating in some way. One thing I notice with a lot of new filmmakers is that they leave some of their best work for 5,

10, or 20 minutes into the feature film. It's unlikely that anyone will stick with the film long enough to get to "the good stuff." Lead with your great material. Perhaps start your story right at "the good part."

41. O - Offer something of value.

When you're thinking about your feature film, think of how you can make the film uniquely valuable to your audience. For example, one time a colleague wanted me to show his film's poster to a film industry notable. I did so, and the filmmaker was disappointed with the result. The notable was not impressed, and it appeared that she thought that the film was just another typical film of a certain genre.

On the other hand, you can do better if you make your film "the first movie to..." A film that gathered a lot of acclaim was *Boys Don't Cry*. Hilary Swank won the Oscar for her portrayal of a young woman who presented herself as a boy. This film was unique, and that helped it stand out. The film was also intense and had a powerful, tragic ending. One value this film offered was to present a stark view of intolerance that is still present in pockets of America.

The next methods are based on the acronym A.U.D.I.O.

42. A - Analyze the most vital information to convey and an emotion to inspire.

You can use audio to save your budget. For example, a character can walk in with his tuxedo and tie askew and say, "Wow! What a party! Bermuda was gorgeous!" With that line of dialogue, you have saved your budget from the expense of location shots of Bermuda. Also, identify the emotion you want to convey. Music or a sound can help you. In one of my feature films, I used a background sound of a wailing baby while a character described a tough situation he survived.

43. U - Understand audio's power as a "bridging" device.

Using a line of dialogue from the next scene to overlap two scenes is an example of an "audio bridge." For example, to make a smooth transition between a farm scene and a scene in New York City, you can have the traffic noise flow in over the shot of a corn field—just before you cut to a shot of the city.

44. D - Divest yourself from the "perfect speakers" error.

Many of us in the film industry mix the audio of a film while listening to the highest quality speakers in the studio. However, we also need to listen to the mix on low-grade consumer speakers. If the audio sounds good on the professional studio speakers it will not necessarily sound good on the web visitor's system. The same goes for how people will hear your film on their television speakers. Even top popular music performers are sure to have some cheap car speakers in the studio to check if their music sounds okay on inferior speakers.

45. I - Investigate your sound engineer's understanding.

A sound engineer will follow your instructions literally, and you must have someone double-check your sound for errors caused by overemphasizing any one element. For example, someone I know told the engineer, "Put the dialogue up front because this project will be judged by men 50 years old and above (who tend to have some hearing loss)." The sound engineer responded literally, and the dialogue was placed too far forward. The sound was terrible because it sounded too artificial. Make sure that you have someone check the sound because by the end of making a film, you may be bleary eyed and "bleary eared" too!

46. O - Open the door to the powerful synergy of audio and video.

The movie *Jaws* has one of the most powerful synergy effects of audio combined with video. This synergetic effect arose due to the problem that the artificial shark kept malfunctioning. So one solution was having the yellow barrels (attached to the submerged shark) rise into the shot with the signature "Da-dum, da-dum" music. With those two elements, the audience knew the shark was present.

* * * * * *

47. Use the methods for coming across as a trustworthy professional.

a) Be on time for appointments.

b) Be accountable and responsible.

c) Turn in projects on time.

d) Ask questions and make sure you get the answers to what you need to know.

e) Devote a lot of effort into being prepared.

f) Provide for your continual education.

g) Focus more on fixing the situation instead of fixing the blame.

h) Develop your people skills; approach problems assertively and avoid acting in an aggressive manner.

48. Compensate for the mistakes of many filmmakers/video producers.

Here are the mistakes many filmmakers/video producers make:

a) NOT knowing their tendencies
b) NOT compensating for their tendencies
c) NOT having a team member who has different artistic preferences voice her opinions
d) NOT having people with faster/slower cutting styles view the rough cut

49. Use a "Statement of Purpose."

As a digital filmmaker, you will be conveying the essence of your project to the media and team members. You'll always be responding to the question, "A movie? What's it about?" Part of your answer can be a Statement of Purpose, which is released to the public and stakeholders in the firm producing the program.

50. Use a "Statement of Artistic Purpose."

When you gather your team, you might use a Statement of Artistic Purpose, which is a few sentences that include the motivating elements (innovation or recognition) for team members. Often, artists like to be doing the first expression of something. For example, a feature film can be "the first movie to show how women recover their self-esteem and personal power after surviving an assault using the Tri-strength system of self-defense."

51. Use a "Statement of Benefits"

This statement is composed of a few sentences that detail the positive outcomes for the audience. Here's an example: "Winter Nights is the first film to express in narrative form the difficulties of both seasonal affective disorder combined with alcoholism. This film increases awareness and inspires additional funding for research in this area."

52. Use the value of testing

Test everything: your logo, your catch phrase, your script (by using a staged reading) and more.

Testing can help you in these areas:

a) See if the idea was successfully communicated.

b) Save your money, save your time.

c) Help you focus the project.

d) Help target your audience.

53. Plan your artistic justification.

Artistic justification is a well-thought out reason for an unusual artistic choice. Let's say you have only a few movie lights to illuminate a scene. Plan a reason for low amount of light in the scene. Perhaps the villain has disengaged the house's power. Now, having a low level of light becomes artistically justified, and the viewers will accept it.

54. Use "Video safe."

Video safe refers to the area of video that is visible on any monitor. The important thing is to frame your shot so that important information is placed away from the edges of the screen so that any monitor can reveal what you want seen.

55. Use Steven Spielberg's comment about a good director.

Spielberg said, "A good director knows when to say 'yes'." Yes, to what? To suggestions about wardrobe, makeup, camera angles, acting choices and a myriad of other possibilities. I add: "A good director creates a warm atmosphere so that there's a lot to say 'yes' to."

* * * * * *

Snatch Victory from the Jaws of Production Defeat (What to do when the shots don't turn out how you want them to)

The following is a brief overview of solutions you can use when you are disappointed with what you filmed. Think of this as a Quick List. These items were included in the Final Exam I gave my digital filmmaking students at Cogswell Polytechnical College in Silicon Valley.

Editing Solutions to Filming Problems:

1. Reframe the shot.

To reframe is to adjust the frame of the image of your shot. You can use your digital editing software to zoom-in to eliminate distracting shadows for example. Television and the Internet are often referred to as "close-up mediums." That is, since the screen is smaller, a close-up shot provides more impact.

In addition, be careful about how far you zoom in. At a certain point, the pixels start to get distracting.

2. Add motion.

You can use your digital editing software to do a zoom-in or a pan across the image of your shot. You can adjust the shot to do both types of motion at the same time. A number of documentaries make a photograph "come alive" by a zoom-in or a pan-across motion.

3. Use sound to cover some error or add A.D.R. or atmosphere.

Often, sound can be your Band-aid solution. For example, one error could be that not enough extras arrived on a particular day. You can film the shots closer in and later add atmosphere—the sounds of clinking glasses and conversation to give us the illusion that the scene takes place in a crowded restaurant. You can add A.D.R. (Automatic Dialogue Replacement), which means to add dialogue in the sound studio. With A.D.R., you can add a crucial bit of dialogue that helps you fill in a gap in the script.

4. Use music.

Let's say you have a romantic scene between the leading man and woman. The dialogue didn't go as planned. You can use music and a few shots of the two people walking and talking to imply that they are becoming closer.

5. Cutaway fast.

To cutaway is to edit so that the shot you are on is shorter. George Lucas used quick cuts in the original release of *Star Wars: A New Hope (Episode IV)* (the first feature film starring Mark Hamill, Harrison Ford and Carrie Fisher). George Lucas cut away from a matte painting after a second or two so the audience would not have time to realize "Oh, that's not real; it's just a painting of parked space ships." Our goal is to give just an impression of the idea or image. Cutaway fast also when you have a weak actor. For example, let's say you need to show a surprise reaction shot. If your actor overacts, cut the shot early when their eyes are just starting to go wide in surprise.

6. Cut on the action (hide the cut).

Here's an example of hiding the cut. In a wideshot, a waiter walks past a table. In a closer shot, the waiter is seen walking past again. When putting these two shots together, you can make the cut feel "seamless" (or hide the cut), by having the waiter begin a move in the wideshot and complete it in the medium shot.

7. Use a visual motif.

The feature film *Mash* appeared like a jumbled, episodic mess in the first rough cut. Then director Robert Altman added the visual motif of the loud speakers as "the glue" between sections. This gave the film unity and rhythm. In one of my feature films, we used a rose as a continuing visual motif.

8. Devise your pick up shot (use a stand-in).

In my feature film that went to the Cannes Film Festival market, the lead actress was unavailable for a reshoot. I had another actress work as a stand-in. In the final edit, I had a shot of the lead actress walk in the door. Then there was a close-up in which the leading man looked up. Then, an over-the-shoulder shot showed the stand-in's back. It became a great opportunity to see the leading man's reaction to the new line created in the editing room: "I've been rehearsing this act for a show. I don't know if it works. Would you be my first audience?"

9. Revisit your throughline

The throughline of your project is the "spine" of the script. For the original *Star Wars* film, it was "make preparations and then destroy the Death Star."

If your rough cut is not working, revisit your throughline. Perhaps too much time has passed between moments where the audience is reminded: "this is what is at stake here."

Here is an example of making a film work by revisiting the throughline. For one of my films, I added a scene in which the main character "David" calls his sweetheart from a payphone. An element of the throughline is that David must tell her that he is out of remission from the disease he suffers. But he stops himself and says, "Oh, there's my bus."

There is no bus, and "David" (and the audience) is disappointed in him.

10. Revisit Your bookends.

Bookends are the process of beginning your project with a startling opening image, and then completing the project with a final image that is a twist on the original image. Here's an example. For one of my films, I began with the image of a man's face as the character falls onto a concrete sidewalk. In the next shot, he gets up, apparently okay. At the end of the film, I show the original shot of the man falling on the sidewalk. The twist is now there is a growing puddle of blood issuing from the man. The shot was further intensified by falling rain. Apparently, the whole film was a glimpse of the man's final, imaginative thoughts before his death.

When you revisit your bookends, you identify what your "twist" is and you think of some images you can place in the middle of your project that support your film's conclusion.

11. Borrow from another scene or from trims or outtakes.

One of my favorite transitions in my feature film that went to the Cannes Film Festival market utilizes an outtake. We filmed a scene with a car coming towards the camera at night. The headlights flashed the camera. I used that flash as a transition to a morning shot. Here's how it went: a) exterior shot of car coming towards the camera, b) flash of headlights, c) additional bright white light added in editing, and d) flash of white dissolves away to reveal the car's interior with the driver talking to his companion the next morning.

Here is an example of borrowing from a trim (excess footage cut from a shot). In *Field of Dreams*, the director Phil

Alden Robinson needed a shot of Ray Liotta looking upon Kevin Costner in an expectant way. Phil did not have the reaction shot. He borrowed a trim from a shot where Ray was just getting ready to catch a baseball. Cut into the scene, the shot now makes it look like Ray's body language is telling Kevin: "Well, what's it going to be? Are you going to take action? I'm ready if you do take action."

12. Use a match cut or montage.

You create a match cut when you use a motion or shape from two different locations to make a smooth cut. You match the motion or shape. On one project, I wanted to connect two different chase scenes. In the first shot the hero is running from a speeding motorcycle. In the second shot, the hero rides a jet ski chased by a pursuing jet ski. The match cut begins with the hero looking back at the motorcycle, then CUT, and the hero completes turning his head to look forward (but now he's on the jet ski with a different pursuer).

A montage is similar to how a number of music videos use a sequence of shots. You cut images together to give an impression such as: "The man and woman are devoting time together and becoming close friends." Many feature films have a song (of course, on the music soundtrack album!) placed over a montage.

You can use this Quick List to bring up your spirits when you feel disappointed when viewing the dailies or rushes (unedited footage) of your project. The above 12 Solutions can help you make your project work.

As a coach, I support a number of my acting clients who take control of their career and produce a project to give their careers a powerful boost. The best to you with your projects.

In the next section, *BOOK III: Self-Promotion for the Actor,* we will cover 25 secrets that you can use to promote yourself and take your career to a higher level.

BOOK III: SELF-PROMOTION FOR THE ACTOR

25 Secrets of Self-Promotion for Actors

Secret #1: Promote constantly.

We have no idea whose sister, uncle or cousin is in the film business. So let people know that you're an actor. Often, someone replies, "Oh, my brother's friend is an actor."

You can reply: "Great. You know, in the film business everyone likes to network. Perhaps I could connect your brother's friend with someone in my network. How do I connect with your brother's friend?"

If you don't promote yourself or focus on networking, you risk having your career fizzle out. One major Hollywood star who refused to network outside of his own expatriate community, Bela Lugosi, fell on hard times. Lugosi had a distinguished career back in Hungary and in fact made many films—even in his heyday, he played many a scientist, a comic relief, a foreign spy, and more. Yet he never went out and schmoozed with Hollywood producers, directors and casting agents. He preferred to stay among his fellow Hungarians, eating the food they liked and listening to native music. When times went bad (after horror movies fell from favor), who did he have batting for him? Almost no one. He ended his days working for Ed Wood, the director of *Plan 9 From Outer Space,* dubbed the worst movie ever made by authors Michael and Harry Medved. Wood was posthumously awarded the Medveds' Golden Turkey Award as the worst director ever.

But this is not for you. Promote constantly, be pleasant to work with and take action to support your own career.

Secret #2: Promote gently.

Listen first; hear the person out. Then sprinkle details about yourself. Do not give someone a two-minute recital of your resume. Just add one detail and then ask the person a question.

Here are helpful questions:

- So how do you know our host?
- What brings you to this conference?
- I'm curious . . . What are you looking forward to?

Here's an example of "sprinkling a detail":

David: "Hey, these desserts look amazing.

Sarah: "Yes. I'm going to have to be good and only choose one. So what do you do?"

David: "I'm an actor. I recently enjoyed playing the lead in a feature film *One Rough Night*. So how do you know our host, Mark?"

You can see how David asks a question and turns the

attention back to Sarah.

Secret #3: Get an insider to believe in you.

"If you're looking to break in, you need to find someone who really believes in you," said James Orr, a top screenwriter. I can testify to the truth of this idea. When I first entered the film industry, I had a screenplay that impressed the then-California Motion Picture Commissioner. For my first feature film, he secured the free use of an American Eagle Airplane and the San Luis Obispo Airport for a scene. He told me that he had been impressed by my screenplay. He said, "Nobody writes like this [with so much heart] anymore."

Secret #4: Ask for the person's gmail.com or yahoo.com email address.

People seem to feel comfortable in giving out an email address at gmail.com or yahoo.com.

Toward the end of your conversation with a new contact, you could say something such as: "It's been great talking with you. How can we stay in contact? Do you have a card?" Then the person replies: "I just ran out of cards." Then you pull out a 3x5 index and say, "Oh, I'll make you a card. Do you have email at gmail or yahoo?" If they don't have a gmail or yahoo address, they usually give you their email address, anyway.

Secret #5: Consider a custom tie

Best-selling author Harvey Mackay wore a shark tie, related to promoting his book *Swim with the Sharks Without Being Eaten Alive.*

Secret #6: Consider a custom button

If you are in a short film, consider having a custom button made. It is a great conversation starter. Perhaps this type of wording would work: "I portrayed Joe in the film *One Rough Night*."

Secret #7: Carry your headshots plus resume with you at all times

You never know whom you might meet. You might meet the cousin of a director while standing in line at a department store. At a networking event, people often do not like to carry full-size materials, so you could have postcards in your pocket, in addition to your business card that has your photo on it.

Secret #8: Carefully use referrals.

Let's realize that some people who say, "Sure, use my name" may not have a positive relationship with the person you want to connect with. Ask, "Oh, how do you know her?"

Somewhere during the conversation, you can also gently ask, "Oh, so how did your last get-together with [contact person] go?" Watch the person's body language to gain clues as to the nature of their relationship.

Secret #9: Smoothly ask for a referral.

Use the phrase: "Who do you know who…" This is an effective phrase because you are clearly asking for what you want. It's also better than saying, "Do you know anyone who might…?" because that is so vague and unsure that it almost invites a reflexive no response.

The next step is to help the person find the right memory. Picture that a person's memory is a room of filing cabinets.

Your job is to help the person have a label on a particular drawer and then to open that drawer. I call this helping the person find the right memory file drawer. For example, I'll say, "Who do you know who could use a speaker on the topic of *Be Heard and Be Trusted*?" When the person hesitates, I say, " Perhaps you were talking with someone at a meeting. Maybe at an association…?"

Secret #10: When following up, consider using a demo-page.

The use of the demo-page is an unusual tactic, and it is vital that you only use it when you already have a relationship with the person. All agents and casting directors are expecting that your first contact will include a headshot with a resume attached. Perhaps after a month or two, you can share a demo-page with the person. The demo-page would include images of you from various projects with a caption beneath each image.

Secret #11: Get people involved with you.

One person can only do so much. That's why it really pays to become the leader of a project. For example, if you create a short video, you can place your image and two other actors on a poster of the video. You can expect that the other actors will send copies of the image via email to other people.

Secret #12: Get other people promoting you.

At one point, I wanted to get feedback about two potential posters for one of my feature films. The father of the little girl who had a role in the film sent via email over 50 copies of the poster concepts to people that he knew. In essence, he was promoting his daughter, and me, and the feature film. This worked well for all of us.

Secret #13: Do something to be associated with the Big Players.

You want the Big Players to know you and to respect you. Here's an example: feature film director Nicholas Meyer first became known as the author of the book, *The Making of LOVE STORY* [the movie]. Then he wrote The Seven Percent Solution, a book about a

fictional meeting between Sherlock Holmes and Dr. Sigmund Freud. Subsequently, Nicholas Meyer directed *Time After Time*. This was a film that Steven Spielberg (Executive Producer) and Robert Zemeckis (co-screenwriter and director) acknowledged viewing when they were preparing *Back to the Future*.

Nicholas Meyer went on to direct *Star Trek II: The Wrath of Khan* and *Star Trek VI: The Undiscovered Country*. We can see that he had entry to the business through his writing efforts.

Here's another example. Lawrence Kasdan began in the film industry when his script for *The Bodyguard* was sold to Warner Bros. as a vehicle for Diana Ross and Steve McQueen. The script only found a home after 37 rejections. The script was finally produced as a 1992 film starring Whitney Houston and Kevin Costner.

Kasdan sold his screenplay Continental Divide to Steven Spielberg, and then George Lucas commissioned Kasdan complete the screenplay for *Star Wars: The Empire Strikes Back (Episode V)*. Lucas then hired Kasdan to write the screenplay for *Raiders of the Lost Ark* and the last installment of the original *Star Wars* trilogy, *Return of the Jedi*. Kasdan made his directing debut in 1981 with *Body Heat*, which he also wrote and which George Lucas quietly helped get produced. It's reported that George Lucas felt that as the creator of *Star*

Wars, it was better to keep a low profile about the sensual *Body Heat* film.

To connect with top players, I interview them and write articles and books based on the interviews. For example, I interviewed Lynda Obst, the producer of *The Siege* (starring Denzel Washington); *Sleepless in Seattle* (Meg Ryan and Tom Hanks) and more. More recently, I interviewed casting directors and others for this book.

Secret #14: Get a photo of yourself on every set on which you perform.

It helps for you to get a photo of yourself on every set on which you perform. These photos are great for postcards. People get tired of repeated viewings of one particular image (like your headshot). More importantly, you create the impression that you're always working.

Secret #15: Consider being the host on a public access TV show.

Someone I know has a public access TV show in which he interviews independent filmmakers. I have been interviewed on his show. He asked me, "Can I give you my headshot?" I replied, "Yes." Many independent filmmakers know him. He stands out from hundreds of other actors.

Secret #16: Create a reason to interview agents, producers, directors or casting directors.

Writing a book gets you access to thousands of people. It does appeal to the vanity of many people to be asked for an interview.

Secret #17: Be careful about E-zines and the frequency of email with Top People.

I use different email lists. When I contact actors, I use one list. For the celebrities that I know, I use another list. I must be careful not to contact celebrities too often. They are extremely busy and prefer to be deleted from many lists.

Secret #18: Keep reminding people how you can be in their project.

I was seeking a role in a film by another director I know. I suggested three different potential roles over the space of weeks by using email and telephone conversations.

Secret #19: Approach each person as a "benevolent detective."

Ask a couple of gentle questions to find out what the person's goals are and to see how you might be helpful to them. I often ask, "How can I be supportive of what you're doing?" And people tell me!

Secret #20: Try one more time.

One time I had a misunderstanding with someone in the entertainment business. I contacted the person with something that could help the person's business. Thereafter, our relationship was in good shape.

Secret #21: Speak their language.

For every group, there is the insider's language. For example, all actors and casting directors refer to sides. Sides are pages of dialogue that include your character's lines. Purchase a book on movie set terminology, study it and memorize the terms.

Secret #22: Carefully use humor.

A certain actor gets more parts because a number of casting decision-makers have his postcard on their desks and office walls. In the photo he is sitting in a bathtub with a cigar in his mouth and a *Variety* newspaper (a trade paper) in his hands.

Secret #23: Consider giving two business cards.

Only give two business cards if you feel you have created enough rapport with the person. This is tricky stuff.

One effective technique is to give one card. Then, when the person says something such as "I'll give this to my brother," you can respond, "Great. And this card is for you. I look forward to staying in contact with you."

Secret #24: Create Welcomed Follow-up.

For busy film industry professionals, some forms of follow-up are like the annoying attacks of a mosquito. For example, some professionals get annoyed about too many phone calls. Top marketing expert Dan Kennedy talks about turning your efforts into those of an invited guest. I call this the process of Welcomed Follow-up. It's based on what the film professional needs. A film producer/director needs information about festivals and distribution.

What does an agency need? More clients. Ask, "Who is your ideal client?" Then look to your network of contacts. Who do you know who works in a big firm? Call her up and ask to be connected with the person who decides on their advertising projects. At an appropriate time, you can connect the contact person in the firm with the agency director.

Secret #25: Learn how to influence people

In my book *Be Heard and Be Trusted,* I share these principles of influence:

You influence people when...

a) They know how much you care.

b) They feel you have common feelings, concerns, and traits.

c) They look on you as a trusted, confident advisor.

Keep these elements in mind, and you can gently influence others.

BOOK IV: SELF-PROMOTION AND HOW TO DO WELL ON TELEVISION AND RADIO (AND WHEN AND HOW TO USE PHOTOS WITH BIG STARS)

Some authors write about techniques for appearing on television and radio in a theoretical way. Not me. I'm writing from experience.

Techniques for Performing Well on Television

1. Look at the host (except certain situations).

Many interviews occur in which you sit across from the host. In that case, you appear natural when you direct your attention to the host. The video camera is just a witness to your conversation with the host. However, some interviews occur when you're in one studio and the host is in another city (in another studio). In that case, you will be advised to look at the camera. I suggest that you practice with your own video camera so that you get used to addressing a camera directly.

2. Be sure to appear attentive to anyone who is speaking.

You never know when the camera is on you for a reaction shot. It looks terrible if your eyes are wandering to look at the audience or cameras. Look at the speaker, and nod your head when appropriate. Be genuine and smile in response to another person's humor. Make sure your face looks alive. Don't let your face fall into a frown.

3. Practice ahead of time.

When best-selling author Harvey Mackay wanted to make the best impression on the CNN Larry King Live television show, Harvey hired and rehearsed with a professional radio interviewer. Harvey's appearance on Larry's show shot his book to the top of the New York Times List of Bestsellers.

4. Bring a sheet with questions.

You can ask the host if she'd like to look at the page of usual questions that you tend to be asked.

5. Watch a number of episodes of the show.

Harvey Mackay watched 18 episodes of the CNN Larry King Live television show in preparation for his appearance.

6. Avoid stripes in your clothing.

Stripes will create a video buzzing pattern on television, caused by how the image is encoded. Avoid stripes and you'll eliminate that distracting pattern.

7. Avoid white shirts or blouses.

The technical people at the television station will need to

darken the image to bring down the contrast created by a white shirt. You will appear less alive. If your complexion is tanned or dark, your face will also appear less distinct.

8. Avoid red in your wardrobe.

Red can appear on television to "bleed"—that is, cause a slight afterimage or streaks across the screen. Avoid red.

9. Bring copies of your book or audio program.

If you choose to gain some celebrity by writing book, be sure to bring copies. Why? Some staff member may misplace your book. Hand your copy to the host before the show so she can hold it up to the camera at the appropriate time.

* * * * * *

The first time I was on radio, KCBS, the interviewer, Jim, asked me pointed questions. It was a stressful time. But it was more stressful for my then-girlfriend, who shook with tension because she was so worried. At home, she didn't know that I had a pen and table full of 3x5 cards so that I could easily keep track of what I wanted to say in response to Jim's severe questions. In fact, I said a couple of times, "I want to go back to that idea you mentioned a couple moments ago . . ."

Techniques for Performing Well on Radio

1. Use notes.

The audience cannot see you. Look at your notes about what points you want to make. And have a note about repeating your 800 phone number.

2. Have an 800 number and repeat it yourself.

What counts is that listeners can reach you. See if you can form words like 800-SOUPBOOK (for the bestselling *Chicken Soup for the Soul* series). You must repeat your 800 number on your own during the interview. Do not count on the host repeating your phone number. That's not her job. She is focused on making the interview interesting. You must promote yourself gently and appropriately.

3. Make the 800 number easy to remember.

If possible, make the 800 number easy to remember like 800-SOUPBOOK.

4. Go back to a topic if appropriate.

Your listeners want to hear you handle topics as they come up. When you answer a question effectively, people are more likely to buy your product or call you. In the middle of the interview, you can use comments such as:

- "Oh Sam, before we go on, I'd like to go back to your comment about ____."
- "A detail that I want to add to this is ____"

5. Get a photo of you in the radio control room.

We are creating social proof that you are an exceptional performer in many arenas. So get a photo of you and the interviewer in the radio control room. Then include it in your press kit.

* * * * * *

How to Get Photos with Big Stars and When to Use Them

1. Offer to take a photo for someone.

One time, I was on a major film set, and I had to ask three different women (extras): "Would you like a photo with [star's name]?" Two of the women were too shy.

Here is the pattern you use when you approach a big star:

Janet: "Hello [star's first name], would you take a photo with her?"

Big Star: "Sure."

[Take the photo.]

Janet: "Oh, [star's first name], how about a photo for me..." [Then, hand your still camera to the person who just had her photo taken.]

2. Approach in a friendly, smooth way (avoid showing nervousness).

You must put the star at ease. Say, "Hi George, would you take a photo with her?" Or use this phrase: "How about a quick photo with her?"

MAJOR WARNING ABOUT TAKING PHOTOS ON THE SET and THE PROCESS FOR SAFELY TAKING PHOTOS:

a) Take photos in a disruptive manner, and you could be thrown off the set. Do not interrupt the flow of filming.

b) Take photos only during a genuine lull in the action. Perhaps take photos during lunch.

c) Keep the camera put away and out of sight. Only take it out briefly. Get photos in

the space of three minutes. Then put the camera away. Don't take it out more than once—don't get greedy!

d) Remember: NO video cameras. Your video camera is likely to be confiscated and the memory card seized.

e) Take a quick amateur snapshot. Do not have a big, sophisticated camera with an ostentatious flash unit on it. Then it appears that you're an uninvited professional

photographer who is going to exploit the photos. If you forgot your camera, purchase a disposable one.

f) Be careful of any high tech or proprietary items on the set. On the set of *Bicentennial Man* (starring Robin Williams as a metal robot), I noticed that the cast and crew were warned *not* to photograph the robot suit.

Since you could be thrown off the set, is getting a photo worth the risk? The answer is: each situation is unique, and only your personal intuition can clue you into whether it's safe for you to take a photograph.

When to Use Photos with Big Stars:

1. Get a photo with a name actor on the set.

What is the benefit of having your photo with a name actor on the set? You show that you're a professional who works with top talent. It's credibility by association.

WARNING: Do NOT associate the name actor with a product or an association. Some people have done this innocently by featuring a photo on a website. Just by having a photo on some websites it may appear that the actor is endorsing something. Avoid this situation! The name actor gets paid for endorsements. Be careful. You are only using the photo like a "news item."

2. Put a caption beneath the photo

Use a caption like: "Jane Smith acting with [Big Star] on the set of *One Rough Night*." Or use the phrase "Jane Smith acts in *One Rough Night*. Seen here with [Big Star] during a break in filming."

3. Use the postcards to create the impression that you're always working.

Follow-up is key with casting decision-makers. Use a postcard with a photo of you on the set of various productions, and you create the impression that you're always working. People want people who are wanted. It's the popularity syndrome. On the postcard, place

a handwritten note like: "Susan, I am still excited about the role of Judy in George Shinn's Red Engine Number 11."

4. Recreate an image of you acting—if necessary

Sometimes you are performing in a play, and you're unable to get a still photo. You may want to consider wearing the wardrobe and getting a close-up shot of you. Use a black background if necessary.

5. Always bring a camera with you!

You never know when an opportunity will present itself. You can purchase a modest cost camera that you can attach to your belt or carry in a purse (or use your smartphone). Recently, I was at a friend's office. She is a casting director who is preparing a website. By having a camera for a spontaneous opportunity, I will benefit every time the casting director looks at her website and sees the photo of the two of us in her office. She'll remember me, and I'll be one step closer to being cast in another production. By the way, she will look at her website every time she inspects changes that her webmaster has completed. So this improves my chances to be on her mind when new acting opportunities come to her attention.

* * * * * *

The Full Interview with Casting Director Randi Acton:

Special Note: In this interview, Randi Acton speaks about parents and child-actors. However, there is much that any actor can gain from the straight forward advice Randi gives.

Tom: What are the mistakes that the child needs to avoid?

Randi: Well, not being prepared. That's probably number one. Not being themselves, trying to act like an actor they've seen on TV, or in a movie. They think they should act like another person. They need to really act like themselves, and just deliver those lines from their heart. [Another mistake is] being nervous for absolutely no reason. Children shouldn't be intimidated by the people that are observing them. The way to prevent that is to just be in front of the camera at home as much as possible. Do an on-camera video diary at home. Put the camera in a room and have them talk to the camera like it's their best friend. So when they go in front of a camera for an audition they relate [well] to the camera.

T: What are the mistakes that the parents need to avoid?

R: Parents make a lot of mistakes. They get extremely pushy, demanding, and sometimes rude. Even if the kid's really talented, and wonderful to work with, we [must] directly work with their parents. If the parents are difficult for us to work with, unfortunately for the child, we don't call them. I mean, this is reality….

I tell parents here [at Break-A-Leg Academy] that they really need to be educated about the business. They need to learn the terminology for themselves so they can help their kid understand on-set terminology. They need to know the difference between a casting director, an agent and a manager. They need to know who gets a percentage and who doesn't.

Parents need to know what they should do and what they shouldn't do. They shouldn't harass the casting director. They shouldn't expect casting people to return calls. If you happen to catch them in the office, they'll talk to you, but they don't call you back if you leave a message saying, "How did my kid do at the audition?" We have no time to call people back. Parents get mad, but they have to understand that if we spent all day calling parents back on how great or not great their kid was, then we're not bringing in the jobs to cast their kids. So they need to understand why we don't. It's not that we're being rude. They just need to understand the business more than they do.

T: What would be the ideal qualifications for a child?

R: The kids [need to be] very comfortable with who they are. It's walking in with confidence, not with their head down. They need to walk with their head up, being just proud of who they are. It's very important that they look you in the eye. So it's not being afraid of making eye contact. They need to just be comfortable in their body, so even dance classes and stuff like that will help them be comfortable. [Children need to] continually get up in front of the whole family at parties and sing a song, do a poem, or read out loud in front of everybody. [They need to] learn to drop the book [so it is not in front of their face]. It should be a daily routine. Ten minutes a day, they work on their craft. It's really just working on who they are, and being themselves.

T: What are ideal qualifications for parents?

R: Parents need to be cooperative. Just pleasant to work with. The entertainment business is extremely stressful and very long hours. Everybody on a production is tired. So when you come on the set you want to be helpful and even share your information with the other parents. Most parents won't help other parents because they're afraid that the other kid will get a part and 'my kid won't.' So people get really into themselves. Don't be selfish. Explain to the new parents who have never been on a set before so that production people don't have to spend so much time. It should be a team thing on the set. Parents tend to be selfish; all they care about is their kid. So parents need to be more open in helping everybody and helping the production itself. Parents need to keep their kids quiet and bring plenty of things for their kids to do on the set. Be pleasant and cooperative.

T: How can a parent be helpful specifically on the set without interfering with the director?

R: Help, maybe, with keeping everybody calm. Never, ever interrupt the flow of the production. [Never tell] any crew member or any director what to do because you'll never be called back. That's a major no-no – whether it's an independent feature film or a big feature film.

T: Specifically, can the parents help a child with getting a line right or something like that?

R: No. Only if the director asks the parent for input or help, that's fine. But never do it without permission. It's hard for parents to understand that because they're very protective. But the parent [must] stay out of the director's way.

T: Sometimes the child looks at the director, then at the parent, and back and forth.

R: That's why they have parents nearby, but not in visual sight of the child. Stay out of the sight lines. In fact, there are certain labor laws that you have to be within so many feet of your child. One time, on a major feature film, [parents] were in a holding area…

You don't want to be right there. Your child will do a much better job if you're not in their sight-line.

T: If there's only one thing you can tell a child that will help her get the part, what is it?

R: No fear. Absolutely no fear. Just be confident. Nobody can play you, better than you can. No one other person will be able to portray you. You are an individual. So don't try to be anyone else. Just be yourself. I tell kids that there are apples and oranges. And a director, in his head, is looking for an apple. You come in, and you're the most talented, gorgeous, most adorable, charismatic orange. He adores you, but you're not an apple. So, it's not personal. Kids really have to know that if you don't get cast, it doesn't mean you're not talented. It just means you're an orange instead of an apple. It's as simple as that. Sometimes, he's looking for an apple, and you really are an incredible orange, and all of a sudden, he switches in his mind: "I don't want an apple. I changed my mind. I want an orange." And you get the part.

T: That's what happened to me. In two feature films I have directed, the part was written as a boy. And a girl came in—and the role changed to a girl. Both times!

R: I remember! Because what you saw ended up being what you needed. But you didn't know it until you saw it.

T: Tell me about how parents help or hinder their children.

R: Here's a parent-kid experience. On one film project, we auditioned for two days—all day long. We received submissions from very well-known kids. We ended up with a [name actor's son]. It didn't matter that he was the well-known actor's son. "Joey" [not his real name] was just brilliant. So he got the part. We had a big decision to make for the lead girl because the film is really about this girl's life.

We saw some really incredible girls, but we had to match up to the boy's age.

We get this girl that's just incredible. And even Joey said, "That's who I want." They had a relationship because they did callbacks together. Their chemistry together was incredible. So everything is perfect. Everything is great. They come to set, and the girl

turns into a complete nightmare. Her acting was brilliant. Her look was great. She became this overnight, stuck-up, little star at a young age. It was a major nightmare. The girl was difficult. Someone went up to her and asked, "What part are you playing?" She replied, "I'm the star!" It got to where we were sick to our stomachs. And her mother didn't handle that at all. Her mother was just as bad. There was a big fight between the mothers.

The really sad thing is only after she grows up and I don't have to deal with her mother, then I will, maybe, audition her. She didn't hurt the film. But it was so difficult on the set, I will never cast her again [as a child]. And I'm sure that the parents have no idea.

It's really sad for the kid. It makes me sad. If the parents are difficult, I will not cast the kid again. We have enough headaches and enough emergency things to deal with. We want to work with actors that are easy to work with. I'd take an actor that is easy to work with even over a talented actor that's a snob. On another film, an adult was complaining about the size of her trailer. She made it a big problem. She was calling her manager in L.A. She is famous, but I won't cast her again. I won't put up with that. There are too many nice people in the world, who are also talented and not stuck-up. I've talked with other casting directors, and most of us don't put up with that.

T: What is one thing you will tell the parents so their

child gets the part?

R: Support your children. Never ever, ever insult them. Never, ever say that wasn't good. Even if they're rotten, you tell them that they're wonderful. You encourage only. You never say, "You did that bad." You never use those words. You say, "How about you be a little louder because I couldn't hear you." Just use positive reinforcement, and say, especially before they go on an audition: "You're great. You're wonderful. And if you don't get the part, I still love you. It doesn't mean anything if you don't get it. It's just the apple and orange thing." You have to tell them the apple and orange story. I continually tell my kids, "Just be yourself."

T: Thank you, Randi.

A FINAL WORD AND THE SPRINGBOARD TO YOUR DREAMS

Congratulations on your efforts with this book.

I'm grateful for this opportunity to provide these insights so you can leap forward to making your dreams come true.

This book is based on a number of workshops I presented. Upon seeing Facebook and email messages of my former college students who were finding it hard to endure as film industry novices, I felt compassion for their plight. I wanted to help them and other actors. So I wrote this book.

We have covered:

1) 21 Darkest Secrets of the Film and Television Industry Every Actor Should Know (and your effective Countermeasures).

2) BOOK II: Taking Control of Your Career: Producing Your Own Short Film, Feature Film or Web Series

3) BOOK III: Self-Promotion for the Actor

4) Book IV: Self-promotion and How to Do Well on Television and Radio (and When and How to Use Photos

with Big Stars)

To gain more value from this book, be sure to go through it and develop your own To Do List. Take some action. Any action towards improving skills and promoting yourself is helpful. I often say, "Better than zero."

Please consider gaining special training through my coaching (phone and in-person), workshops and presentations.

Note the other eight books in this series. . .

- Darkest Secrets of Making a Pitch to the Film and Television Industry
- Darkest Secrets of Film Directing
- Darkest Secrets of Charisma
- Darkest Secrets of Persuasion and Seduction Masters: How to Protect Yourself and Turn the Power to Good
- Darkest Secrets of Business Communication: Using Your Personal Brand
- Darkest Secrets of Small Business Marketing
- Darkest Secrets of Spiritual Seduction Masters
- Darkest Secrets of Negotiation Masters

See my blog at
www.BeHeardandBeTrusted.com

The best to you and may your acting dreams come true.
Tom
Tom Marcoux,
Motion Picture Director, Actor, Producer, Screenwriter
America's Communication Coach
P.S. View the 8 Other *Darkest Secrets* books:
See **Free Chapters** of Tom Marcoux's 19 books

at http://amzn.to/ZiCTRj

Titles include:
Be Heard and Be Trusted
Nothing Can Stop You This Year
Truth No One Will Tell You
10 Seconds to Wealth
Your Secret Charisma
Wake Up Your Spirit to Prosperity
The Cat Advantage
— and more.
(For coaching, reach Tom Marcoux
at tomsupercoach@gmail.com)

EXCERPT FROM
DARKEST SECRETS OF PERSUASION AND SEDUCTION MASTERS: HOW TO PROTECT YOURSELF AND TURN THE POWER TO GOOD

by Tom Marcoux

BOOK I
Darkest Secrets of Persuasion Masters

I never expected to write *Darkest Secrets of Persuasion and Seduction Masters: How to Protect Yourself and Turn the Power to Good.*

But I was angry and I had to stand up for you.

When I was a child, I was hurt badly. My parents could not protect me. As a young man, in one of my first business deals, I was hurt terribly.

Now, I am in my 40's, with gray in my hair, and for 27 years I have been taking action to protect people.

And now is the time for me to protect you with the Countermeasures I reveal in this book.

Every human being needs to be able to
break the trance that a Manipulator

creates. You need to make good decisions
so you are safe and you keep growing
—and you are not cut down and crippled.

This Darkest Secrets material is so intense that I first released it only with the counterbalance of my most energizing and uplifting books, *Nothing Can Stop You This Year!* and *10 Seconds to Wealth: Master the Moment Using Your Divine Gifts.*

An interviewer asked me: "Who can be the Manipulator?"

A co-worker, a boss, a salesperson, someone you're dating, and someone you think is a friend.

Now is the time—this very minute—for me to write this book to protect you.

I must speak the truth.

These darkest secrets of "persuasion masters" are …

Wait a minute! Let's say it plainly: These are the darkest secrets of masters of manipulation. Throughout this book, I will call these people what they are: Manipulators.

Dictionary.com defines "manipulate" as "To influence or manage shrewdly or deviously.... To tamper with or falsify for personal gain."

In this book, we will look on a manipulator as one who deviously influences someone with no concern about that person's well-being, and who causes harm to that person.

Here is the first Darkest Secret:

Darkest Secret #1:
Manipulators Make You Hurt
and Then Offer the Salve.

Manipulators would invite you to go out in the sun for hours and then sell you the salve to soothe your burns. The problem is that we don't notice that this is what they're doing.

For example, you're considering the purchase of a house. A Manipulator asks the question, "So, where would you put your TV?" This question is designed to put you into a trance.

Dictionary.com defines "trance" as "a half-conscious state, seemingly between sleeping and waking, in which ability to function voluntarily may be suspended." Let's condense this: in a trance you may not be able to function freely.

Here is the second Darkest Secret:

Darkest Secret #2:
Manipulators Put You into a Trance.

To protect yourself, you must learn to use *Countermeasures to Break the Trance.*

All the Countermeasures (actions you can take to break the trance) in this book will make you stronger and more capable of protecting yourself.

Now, we'll view the third Darkest Secret:

Darkest Secret #3:
Manipulators Care Nothing for You and Human Decency: They'll lie, cheat, and do whatever they need to do so they win—but their charm masks all this.

Let's return to the example of a Manipulator selling you a house. A Manipulator does not pause for an instant to see if you can truly afford the new house. The Manipulator would neglect to mention that you will not only have your mortgage payment of $900. There will be additional costs: home repairs, property tax, water, electricity, homeowner's insurance, and more. The Manipulator only emphasizes what he or she knows you want to hear: "Look! $900 is better than the $1500 you're paying for rent, which is just going down the toilet. And the $900 is an investment."

Let's go back to **Darkest Secret #1:**

Manipulators make you hurt and then offer the salve.

The Manipulator has you feeling good about the solution (salve) and feeling bad about your current life situation.

How? A Manipulator will make you hurt through questions such as:

- What bothers you about paying $1500 a month for rent? (The Manipulator will use a derisive tone when he says the word rent.)
- What is not smart about paying rent on someone else's house instead of investing in your own house?
- How do you feel about your children walking in the neighborhood where you live now?

Do you see how these questions are designed to make you hurt enough so that you'll buy?

An interviewer asked me, "Tom, aren't these good arguments for purchasing a house?"

"What we're looking at is the intention of the influencer," I replied. "Let's look at our definition of a manipulator as one who deviously influences someone with no concern about that person's well-being, and who causes harm to that person. If the person truly cannot afford the house, he or she will be harmed by buying it. If the manipulator conceals the truth, the manipulator is doing harm. That's the important difference."

Some friends of mine are ethical and helpful real estate agents who truthfully reveal the whole situation and help the purchaser achieve her own goals.

In this book, we are talking about another type of person; that is, unethical Manipulators.

* * *

In any given moment, we need to remember the tactics Manipulators use. We will focus on the word D.A.R.K. so you can remember details easily and protect yourself from Manipulators.

D — Dangle something for nothing
A — Alert to scarcity
R — Reveal the Desperate Hot Button
K — Keep on pushing buttons

We'll begin with *Dangle something for nothing* with the next chapter.

CHAPTER TWO: DANGLE SOMETHING FOR NOTHING

The first method of D.A.R.K. is *Dangle Something for Nothing.*

What do conmen and conwomen do to seize your attention? They make you think you're getting a "steal."

I recently saw a documentary in which a conman on a street in England showed a toy that looked like it was dancing. This fake product was actually dancing because of a hidden, invisible thread. The conman was dangling something for nothing. The Entranced Buyer thought he was getting something worth $20 for only $5. That was the trick. The Entranced Buyer felt that he was getting $15 extra of value for his $5. What the Buyer really got was something worth nothing. Similarly, I know someone who purchased a copy of a Disney movie from a street vendor in San Francisco. She brought the copy home and it was unwatchable—and the street vendor was never seen again.

An old phrase goes, "A conman cannot con someone who is not looking for something for nothing."

How to Protect Yourself from "Dangle Something for Nothing"

Stop! Get on your cell phone and talk through the "deal" with someone you know who thinks clearly. Go home. Think about it. Do some research on the Internet. Listen to your gut feelings. If the salesman or conman is too insistent, get away from that Manipulator. Get quiet. Have a cup of water. Cool down. Break the Trance!

Break the Trance and Identify the Crucial Detail

Earlier, I mentioned that a Manipulator puts you into a trance. An added problem is that we put ourselves into a trance. For example, as you read this, are you thinking about your right toe? Most likely not (unless you stubbed your toe recently). The point is that we only focus on a tiny percentage of what is going on in our life.

Around fifteen years ago, I caused myself trouble because I put myself into a trance. I discovered that under certain conditions, friendship can make you nearly deaf. Here's how: I was producing a song for a motion picture. A good friend was singing backup in the chorus. Because of our friendship, I wanted him to sound great. I completely missed the Crucial Detail. In this kind of situation, the Crucial Detail is that what truly counts is how the lead singer sounds! I made a song that I could not release. What a waste of time and money! I had put myself into a trance.

In any situation in which the Manipulator is "dangling something for nothing," we often fall into a trance and miss the Crucial Detail. The most important detail is not that we're saving money if we order before midnight tonight. What counts is whether the product creates a lasting, crucial benefit in our lives. And is the benefit of the product worth the cost? Some people even program themselves to make mistakes by saying, "I can't pass up a bargain." The bargain is not the Crucial Detail.

Secrets to Break the Trance

This is the process of B.R.E.A.K.S. It will help you remember the proven methods to break a trance.

B — Breathe
R — Relax
E — Envision
A — Act on aromas
K — Keep moving
S — Smile

End of Excerpt from

Darkest Secrets of Persuasion and Seduction Masters: How to Protect Yourself and Turn the Power to Good

ABOUT THE AUTHOR

Tom Marcoux helps people like you fulfill big dreams. Known as America's Communication Coach, Tom has authored 19 books with sales in 15 countries. One of his *Darkest Secrets* books rose to #1 on Amazon.com Hot New Releases in Business Life (and in Business Communication). He guides clients and audiences (IBM, Sun Microsystems, etc.) to success in job interviewing, public speaking, media relations, and branding. A member of the National Speakers Association, he is a professional coach and guest expert on TV, radio, and print, and was dubbed "the Personal Branding Instructor" by the *San Francisco Examiner.* Tom addressed National Assoc. of Broadcasters' Conference six years running. With a degree in psychology, Tom is a guest lecturer at **Stanford University**, DeAnza, & California State University, and teaches public speaking, science fiction cinema/literature and comparative religion at Academy of Art University. Winner of a special award at the **Emmys**, Tom wrote, directed, and produced a feature film that the distributor took to the **Cannes film market**, and the film gained international distribution. He is engaged in book/film projects *Crystal Pegasus* (children's) and *TimePulse* (science fiction). See TomSuperCoach.com and Tom's well-received blog at www.BeHeardandBeTrusted.com

Tom Marcoux can help you with **speech writing** and **coaching for your best performance.**

As Tom says, *Make Your Speech a Pleasant Beach.*

Join Tom's Linkedin.com group: *Executive Public Speaking and Communication Power.*

Get a **Free** report: "9 Deadly Mistakes to Avoid for Your Next Speech and 9 Surefire Methods" at http://tomsupercoach.com/freereport9Mistakes4Speech.html

Tom Marcoux has trained CEOs, small business owners, and graduate students to speak with impact and gain audiences' tremendous approval and cooperation. *Learn how to present and get thunderous applause!*

"Tom, Thanks for your coaching and work with me on revising my speech at a major university. Working with you has been so enlightening for me. Through your gentle prodding and guidance I was able to write a speech that connects with the audience. I wish everyone could experience the transformation I have undergone. You have helped me discover the warm and compelling stories that now make my speech reach hearts and uplift minds. This was truly an empowering experience. I cannot thank you enough for your great assistance." — J.S.

Become a fan of Tom's graphic novels/feature films:

Science fiction: *TimePulse*
www.facebook.com/timepulsegraphicnovel

Fantasy Thriller: *Jack AngelSword*
type "JackAngelSword" at Facebook.com

Children's Fantasy: *Crystal Pegasus*
www.facebook.com/crystalpegasusandrose

See **Free Chapters** of Tom Marcoux's 19 books
at http://amzn.to/ZiCTRj

Special Offer Just for Readers of this Book:

Contact Tom Marcoux at tomsupercoach@gmail.com for special discounts on books, coaching, workshops and presentations. Just mention your experience with this book.

CPSIA information can be obtained at www.ICGtesting.com
Printed in the USA
LVOW04s2145171114

414217LV00012B/369/P

9 780615 809342